D0551769

The Uses of Sociology:
Traditions, Methods and Practices

PEMBROKESHIRE COLLEGE

R17340N0618

Sociology and Society

This book is part of a series of four. The first three are published by Blackwell in association with The Open University. The complete list of books in the course is as follows:

Understanding Everyday Life, edited by Tony Bennett and Diane Watson

Social Differences and Divisions, edited by Peter Braham and Linda Janes

Social Change, edited by Tim Jordan and Steve Pile

The Uses of Sociology: Traditions, Methods and Practices, edited by Peter Redman, Elizabeth B. Silva and Sophie Watson

The Uses of Sociology:
Traditions, Methods and Practices

edited by Peter Redman, Elizabeth B. Silva and Sophie Watson

The Open University

This publication forms part of an Open University course DD201 *Sociology and Society*. Details of this and other Open University courses can be obtained from the Student Registration and Enquiry Service, The Open University, PO Box 625, Milton Keynes, MK7 6YG, United Kingdom: tel. +44 (0)1908 653231, email general-enquiries@open.ac.uk

Alternatively, you may visit the Open University website at http://www.open.ac.uk where you can learn more about the wide range of courses and packs offered at all levels by The Open University.

To purchase a selection of Open University course materials visit http://www.ouw.co.uk, or contact Open University Worldwide, Michael Young Building, Walton Hall, Milton Keynes MK7 6AA, United Kingdom for a brochure. tel. +44 (0)1908 858785; fax +44 (0)1908 858787; email ouwenq@open.ac.uk

The Open University
Walton Hall, Milton Keynes
MK7 6AA

First published 2002. Second edition 2005.

Copyright © 2002, 2005 The Open University

All rights reserved. No part of this publication may be reproduced, stored in a retrieval system, transmitted or utilised in any form or by any means, electronic, mechanical, photocopying, recording or otherwise, without written permission from the publisher or a licence from the Copyright Licensing Agency Ltd. Details of such licences (for reprographic reproduction) may be obtained from the Copyright Licensing Agency Ltd of 90 Tottenham Court Road, London W1T 4LP.

Open University course materials may also be made available in electronic formats for use by students of the University. All rights, including copyright and related rights and database rights, in electronic course materials and their contents are owned by or licensed to The Open University, or otherwise used by The Open University as permitted by applicable law.

In using electronic course materials and their contents you agree that your use will be solely for the purposes of following an Open University course of study or otherwise as licensed by The Open University or its assigns.

Except as permitted above you undertake not to copy, store in any medium (including electronic storage or use in a website), distribute, transmit or retransmit, broadcast, modify or show in public such electronic materials in whole or in part without the prior written consent of The Open University or in accordance with the Copyright, Designs and Patents Act 1988.

Index compiled by Isobel McLean.

Edited and designed by The Open University.

Typeset by The Open University.

Printed and bound in the United Kingdom by the Alden Group, Oxford.

ISBN 0 7492 6826 3

2.1

Contents

The Open University Course Team

Hedley Bashforth, Tutor Panel Member and Author
Melanie Bayley, Media Project Manager and Editor
Tony Bennett, Joint Course Chair, Author and Book Editor
Peter Braham, Author and Book Editor
Kathleen Calder, Editor
Lene Connolly, Print Buying Controller
Margaret Dickens, Print Buying Co-ordinator
Richard Doak, Tutor Panel Member and Author
Molly Freeman, Course Secretary
Richard Golden, Production and Presentation Administrator
Peter Hamilton, Author and Book Editor
Ramaswami Harindranath, Media Author
Fiona Harris, Freelance Editor
Celia Hart, Picture Researcher
Sue Hemmings, Author
David Hesmondhalgh, Media Author
Karen Ho, Course Secretary
Rich Hoyle, Graphic Designer
Jonathan Hunt, Co-publishing Advisor
Denise Janes, Course Secretary
Linda Janes, Author and Book Editor
Yvonne Jewkes, Tutor Panel Member and Author
Tim Jordan, Author and Book Editor
Hugh Mackay, Author
Karl Maton, Tutor Panel Member and Author
Liz McFall, Author
Margaret McManus, Copyrights Co-ordinator
Diane Mole, Graphic Designer
Gerry Mooney, Author
Karim Murji, Author
Janet Parr, Tutor Panel Member and Author
Steve Pile, Author and Book Editor
Winifred Power, Editor
Peter Redman, Joint Course Chair, Author and Book Editor
Roger Rees, Course Manager
Halimeh Sharifat, Course Manager Assistant
Jane Sheppard, Graphic Designer
Norma Sherratt, Author
Elizabeth B. Silva, Author and Book Editor
Lynne Slocombe, Freelance Editor
Kenneth Thompson, Joint Course Chair, Author and Book Editor
Howie Twiner, Graphic Artist
Diane Watson, Author and Book Editor
Sophie Watson, Author and Book Editor
Emma Wheeler, Production and Presentation Administrator
Kathryn Woodward, Author

Consultant Authors

Mitchell Dean, Macquarie University
Celia Lury, Goldsmiths College
Jim McGuigan, Loughborough University
Mike Savage, University of Manchester
Merl Storr, University of East London
Bryan S. Turner, University of Cambridge

External Assessors

Debbie Epstein, University of Cardiff (midlife update)
Rosemary Pringle, University of Southampton

Preface to the series

Sociology and Society is a series of four books designed as an introduction to the sociological study of modern society. The books form the core study materials for The Open University course *Sociology and Society* (DD201), which aims to provide an attractive and up-to-date introduction to the key concerns and debates of contemporary sociology. They also take account of the ways in which sociology has been shaped by dialogue with adjacent disciplines and intellectual movements, such as cultural studies and women's studies.

The first book in the series is *Understanding Everyday Life*, whose aim is to 'defamiliarize' our relations to everyday life by showing how the perspectives of sociology, cultural studies and feminism can throw new light on, and prompt a reflexive attention to, varied aspects of day-to-day social life that are usually taken for granted. The book is designed as a means of illustrating and debating different aspects of everyday life in a number of key sites – the home, the street, the pub, the neighbourhood and community – and in various social activities, such as work and consumption, and teenage romance.

The second book, *Social Differences and Divisions*, in addition to looking at class, which sociologists have treated as one of the central forms of social stratification, also explores social differences and divisions based on gender, 'race' and ethnicity. The book then examines the concepts of citizenship and social justice – concepts that both reflect and influence the perception of social divisions. Finally, the book contains case studies of two key sectors – education and housing – which highlight significant divisions and inequalities; it also looks at the social policies that have been designed to address them.

Social Change, the third book, shows how, from sociology's early concerns with the transition to industrial and democratic social forms to recent debates over the rise of information, networked or global societies, sociology has been centrally concerned with the nature and meaning of social change. However, the book seeks to frame these debates through an explicit examination of the spaces and times of social change. Social transformations are exemplified and questioned by looking at the ways in which societies organize space–time relations. The topics and examples include: urbanism and the rhythms of city life, colonialism and post-colonialism, the alleged transition from industrial to information society, new media and time–space reconfiguration, intimacy and the public sphere, and the regulation of the self. Finally, it examines new perspectives on how sociology itself is implicated in social change.

The last book in the series, *The Uses of Sociology: Traditions, Methods and Practices*, replaces an earlier text, *The Uses of Sociology* edited by Peter Hamilton and Kenneth Thompson. It explores competing approaches to the question, what constitutes authoritative knowledge in society?; introduces the main methods of sociological research; and considers various ways of understanding the purposes of sociology and its relationship to politics, government and commerce.

Although edited volumes, each of the chapters has been specially commissioned for the series in order to provide a coherent and up-to-the minute introduction to sociology. Throughout the chapters, key terms and names are highlighted. These can be further studied by consulting a sociological dictionary, such as *The Blackwell Dictionary of Sociology* or *The Penguin Dictionary of Sociology*. The overall approach taken is interactive, and we hope general readers will use the activities and the questions based on the readings in order to engage actively with the texts.

Peter Redman
Elizabeth B. Silva
Sophie Watson
on behalf of The Open University Course Team

The uses of sociology: introduction

Peter Redman, Elizabeth B. Silva and Sophie Watson

The title of this book, *The Uses of Sociology*, raises an important and challenging question: what is sociology for or, put another way, how can sociology best be used? Perhaps one of the most obvious answers to this question is that sociology is useful in providing us with knowledge about the social world. Elsewhere in DD201 you have been introduced to the particular ways of 'seeing' and thinking that underpin such sociological knowledge. For example, you have explored some of the major phenomena sociologists study (everyday life, social divisions, social change); the characteristic ways in which sociologists approach these phenomena (for instance, 'defamiliarizing' or 'making strange' that which is often taken for granted); and the often competing concepts and theories they use to make sense of them. However, the generation of sociological knowledge involves something in addition to the above, something that is nevertheless embedded in these characteristic ways of seeing and thinking. It involves the use of specific sociological *research methods* and it is these that are at the heart of *The Uses of Sociology* and the wider module of which it is a part.

Sociological research methods have, of course, been present throughout DD201. Many chapters draw extensively on existing research (think, for example, of **Mitchell Dean's (2002)** use of the ground breaking historical studies conducted by Norbert Elias in Chapter 6 of *Social Change* or **Peter Braham's and Norma Sherratt's (2002)** use of research by Gerwitz *et al.* on parental choice and schooling in Chapter 7 of *Social Differences and Divisions*). Others report on research conducted by the chapter authors themselves: for instance, **Diane Watson's (2002)** study of pub cultures and **Elizabeth B. Silva's (2002)** study of everyday routines (in Chapters 5 and 7 respectively of *Understanding Everyday Life*); and **Mike Savage's (2002)** study of attitudes to class (in Chapter 2 of *Social Differences and Divisions*). However, while methods have appeared elsewhere in the course, they have not themselves been the subject of detailed exploration. *The Uses of Sociology* brings these methods into focus, introducing you in an accessible manner to different approaches to sociological research, their strengths and weaknesses, the ethical issues to which these give rise, and the evaluation of sociological research evidence. This does not mean that, as part of *The Uses of Sociology* module, you will be asked to undertake research of your own. Rather, the module aims to give you an appreciation of how sociological research is done so that, when you come across sociological evidence, you will understand how this has been generated and be in a better position to evaluate the conclusions drawn from it.

While reflections about sociological research methods are to be found at the heart of this book – specifically, in Chapters 2 and 3 – their exploration necessarily raises a number of further issues about sociology and its uses. This is because, as tools for generating knowledge, research methods are never simply neutral but are always embedded in competing *outlooks* on the social world. To put this another way, we can say that research methods are informed by competing perspectives or philosophical starting points and that these contain different visions of what constitutes *authoritative* (or 'valid') *knowledge* about the social world, together with different visions of the *purpose* of sociological enquiry. In short, research methods – together with the knowledge they produce – are themselves social products. *The Uses of Sociology* explores these issues in both Chapters 1 and 4.

In Chapter 1, we depart from the question, what constitutes authoritative knowledge about the social world? As such, Chapter 1 asks: should sociology adopt (or adapt) the methods of the natural sciences (chemistry, biology and physics) in pursuit of scientific explanations of the social world or does the nature of the social world mean that we need different methods and a different understanding of what constitutes knowledge from those available in these disciplines? Equally, it asks: what is the nature of the objects of sociological enquiry; can we stand 'outside' them in the detached manner of the natural scientist or are we necessarily and inextricably involved with them; should sociological research aim to be value-free; and, if this is an impossibility, what should sociologists do about their values?

In relation to the wider purposes of sociological research, Chapter 4 asks: should sociological research be confined to the generation of 'pure' knowledge inside the academy; should it be a tool for commerce or the rational organization and administration of society; or, alternatively, should its purpose be explicitly political: to bring about (or prevent) political, social and economic change? In raising these issues, it goes on to ask questions about what happens when sociological methods and forms of knowledge are taken up in other spheres of life such as politics, business and commerce, and social administration. Does sociological knowledge simply reflect the realities of these spheres of life or does it interact with and perhaps even change them?

In the coming weeks, then, you will be exploring important questions about how sociology can best be used to generate authoritative knowledge and about the uses of sociology in relation to the wider world.

Clarifying terms

Before beginning our exploration of sociological research methods and the perspectives and assumptions that inform them it will be as well to reflect on and clarify a number of technical terms – either because these appear throughout the chapters that follow or because they occur frequently in debates in this area.

Perhaps the most obvious place to begin is with the term *research methods*. Research methods can sometimes seem intimidating or arcane. However, they are not wholly divorced from everyday activities. For instance, when we consult bus timetables and road maps, or compare prices of goods and services to ensure we will get the best deal, we adopt systematic procedures in order to find things out. Although sociological research methods are more formalized and more specialized than this, the principle that underlies them is the same. They are systematic, organized, transparent and rigorous procedures for generating and analysing evidence on the basis of which sociologists seek to build authoritative claims about the particular social phenomenon under study.

Research methods are often divided into two kinds: those concerned with generating **qualitative** evidence (or 'data') and those concerned with generating *quantitative* evidence. Quantitative data are those that can be expressed in numerical form – for example, football results, rainfall records, and rates of unemployment. As this begins to suggest, qualitative data can be understood as those not expressed as numerical quantities – for example, transcripts of conversations or television programmes, photographs, or detailed descriptions of everyday social practices (like Goffman's account of handholding discussed in Chapter 3 of *Understanding Everyday Life* (**Hamilton, 2002**)). However, while true, this distinction fails to capture what is perhaps most valuable about data of each kind. One way to think about this is to consider what might be discovered from numerical as opposed to qualitative data about, for example, your favourite foods. Numerical data might tell you how often and how much of this was consumed and by how many people; qualitative data would tell you what it feels like to eat it in different contexts by different individuals. Needless to say, both types of data are valuable and, as subsequent chapters in this volume will argue, although they are rather different and their use often implies diverging philosophical assumptions about the nature of the social world, we would be mistaken if we were to assume that they are somehow in opposition or cannot be combined to produce rich and complex sociological accounts.

In everyday usage, you will often see research methods used interchangeably with the term **methodology**. In sociology, it is more usual to draw a distinction between these terms, with the former being used to refer to the applied techniques and procedures of research, and the latter to the underlying assumptions and analytical structures that inform the choice and use of these methods, together with the process of critical reflection on these. Understood in this way, methodological issues necessarily raise, in their turn, issues of **ontology** and **epistemology**. Put simply, ontology refers to what we believe to exist; epistemology refers to the means by which we have knowledge of this. However, since these definitions are perhaps more difficult to grasp than those already discussed, let's pause for a moment to explore this distinction in more detail.

How, for instance, might we characterize the ontology and epistemology of someone who is religious? Since ontology refers to that which we believe to exist, the first thing we might say is that, depending on the religion in question, his or her ontology will include a belief in the existence of a creator God. Similarly, since epistemology refers to how we have knowledge about that which we believe to exist, the next thing we might say is that his or her epistemology will include adherence to the principle that Holy Scripture provides divine revelation or knowledge of this God. In contrast, if we were asked to characterize the ontology and epistemology of a natural scientist, we might begin by saying

qualitative

methodology

ontology
epistemology

that her or his ontology will include the belief that only that which can be observed and measured can be said to exist and then add that her or his epistemology will include adherence to the principle that knowledge is that which is generated via processes of observation and measurement in which facts and values are kept strictly separate.

In sociology, ontological and epistemological debates frequently focus on questions concerning the issue of what constitutes authoritative sociological knowledge. For example, whether the objects of sociological enquiry can be considered to exist as objective entities equivalent to those studied by natural scientists (an ontological question) or whether, in the generation of sociological knowledge, researchers should seek to remain detached from or be involved with the people they are studying (an epistemological question).

Outline of the chapters

Chapter 1, *'In search of authoritative sociological knowledge'* introduces you to these ontological and epistemological debates by exploring two of the major traditions that have informed sociological research – 'positivism' and 'interpretivism'. In introducing these, the chapter makes preliminary links between them and different methods of sociological research and raises questions about whether sociological research should aim to be detached from or involved in its objects of study; whether it is possible to keep facts separate from values in sociological research; and whether sociological research should seek to explain or understand the social world. These oppositions – between *detachment/involvement, facts/values*, and *explanation/understanding* – thus form an important organizing framework for the chapter as a whole.

Chapter 2, *'Qualitative sociological research'* introduces you to some of the central methods for generating and analysing qualitative data. The chapter addresses the ontological and epistemological issues particular to qualitative approaches and introduces you to qualitative interviewing techniques, ethnography, and the evaluation of documentary and visual evidence. Drawing on examples from across DD201, as well as additional material, the chapter provides you with a chance to do some 'hands on' analysis of visual data; explores the strengths and weaknesses of qualitative approaches to data generation and analysis; and considers the ethical issues to which these give rise. The chapter concludes by addressing issues of validity and generalizability in qualitative research.

Chapter 3, *'Quantitative sociological research'* addresses methods of generating and analysing quantitative data, focusing in particular on one of the main tools for quantitative social research: the social survey. This method is often associated with a more 'positivist' tradition (as discussed in Chapter 1) but, as Chapter 3 argues, in practice, such distinctions often break down. The chapter argues that quantification is also a part of the social world and what 'counts' in numbers is not a neutral and 'objective' matter. As in Chapter 2, you will have the opportunity to do some 'hands on' activities, as well as to explore the strengths and weaknesses of quantitative methods, and the ethical issues to which they give rise.

Finally, *The Uses of Sociology: Traditions, Methods and Practices* concludes, in Chapter 4, **'The purposes and practices of sociology'** by asking what the purpose of sociological research should be – the generation of knowledge about the social world; a tool for commerce or social administration; or an instrument of political change? In so doing, it explores what happens when sociological research findings leave the academy and enter other spheres of life.

The Uses of Sociology and DD201

The Uses of Sociology: Traditions, Methods and Practices, is the course book accompanying *The Uses of Sociology* module in the current version of DD201. It incorporates material from an earlier version of the course, specifically: *The Uses of Sociology* edited by Peter Hamilton and Kenneth Thompson (2002), and the 'DD201 Methods Booklets 1–4' by Janet Parr. You will sometimes see these items referred to in this volume (and elsewhere in the course materials). The Hamilton and Thompson volume is also on sale in book shops. However, you *are not* required to read these items as part of your studies for DD201.

As elsewhere in the course, terms highlighted in bold in the text can be pursued further by looking them up in *The Penguin Dictionary of Sociology* or similar publications.

Learning objectives

In summary, your learning objectives for *The Uses of Sociology* module are to develop:

1   knowledge and understanding of the competing perspectives on what, in the context of sociological research, constitutes authoritative knowledge, and on what the purpose of sociological research should be;

2   an introductory knowledge and understanding of the sociological methods used to generate and analyse qualitative and quantitative data; the ethical issues to which these give rise; how they relate to issues of validity and generalizability; and some of the strengths and weaknesses of these approaches to sociological research;

3   an introductory knowledge and understanding of issues arising from the evaluation of sociological research evidence; and

4   familiarity with some of the ways in which sociological knowledge and research methods have informed other spheres of life (such as politics, commerce, and social policy and administration).

As elsewhere in DD201, what you get out of the module will depend on the amount you are able to put into your studies – in particular, with regards to the depth and breadth of reading you are able to undertake; the extent to which you engage with the Activities; and your ability to build up an overall picture of the module and its relationship to the rest of DD201 via detailed note-taking.

References

Bennett, T. and Watson, D. (eds) (2002) *Understanding Everyday Life*, Oxford, Blackwell/The Open University.

Braham, P. and Janes, L. (eds) (2002) *Social Differences and Divisions*, Oxford, Blackwell/The Open University.

Braham, P. and Sherratt, N. (2002) 'Education, housing and social justice' in Braham, P. and Janes, L. (eds) *op. cit*.

Dean, M. (2002) 'The regulation of the self' in Jordan, T. and Pile, S. (eds) *Social Change*, Oxford, Blackwell/The Open University.

Hamilton, P. (2002) 'The street and everyday life' in Bennett, T. and Watson, D. (eds) *op. cit*.

Hamilton, P. and Thompson, K. (2002) *The Uses of Sociology*, Oxford, Blackwell/The Open University.

Savage, M. (2002) 'Social exclusion and class analysis' in Braham, P. and Janes, L. (eds) *op. cit*.

Silva, E. B. (2002) 'Gender and routines in narratives of everyday life in families' in Bennett, T. and Watson, D (eds) *op. cit*.

Watson, D. (2002) '"Home from home": The pub and everyday life' in Bennett, T. and Watson, D. (eds) *op. cit*.

In search of authoritative sociological knowledge

Peter Redman

Contents

1   Introduction

Writing about the uses of sociology, Peter Hamilton and Kenneth Thompson described the following incident:

> On 18 April 2001, the most authoritative French newspaper, *Le Monde*, published a front-page article under the title 'Sociology under a bad star'. In the article, two sociologists fulminated, in the name of scientific rigour, against the damage that might be done to the reputation of the discipline by the award of a university doctorate to a media astrologer, who had successfully submitted a sociological thesis on astrology. Not only was this considered a sufficiently important issue for *Le Monde* to concern its readers with, but it was responded to by the rival newspaper, *Libération* (19 April 2001). The sociologist writing the full-page article in *Libération* [Alain Bourdin] pointed out that, although it was permissible to raise the question of whether scientific distance had been respected in such a thesis, it had to be recognised that there had been some excellent theses on the sociology of religion by Catholic priests. However, his concern was that the professional and scientific status of sociology might be endangered by debating this issue in the media. He concluded, echoing Comte, that sociology ('and French sociology remains one of the best') has a considerable richness that might be jeopardised as 'an instrument for organizing the present and imagining the future'.
>
> (Hamilton and Thompson, 2002, p.xi)

Seen from the UK, where the media rarely discuss sociology as a discipline, the prominence given to this debate may appear surprising. However, for our current purposes, its interest lies less in what it might tell us about national differences in media reporting of sociology than in what it suggests about the central question running through this chapter: namely, what constitutes authoritative sociological knowledge?

Among the most notable features of both the original *Le Monde* article and Bourdin's response to this were the authors' commitment to keeping facts separate from values (this was the major concern of the original *Le Monde* article – that a sociological study of astrology by a practising astrologer would be inherently biased); their espousal of sociology's scientific status; and their belief

JEUDI 19 AVRIL 2001

Rebonds

En donnant le titre de docteur à une astrologue médiatique, le monde universitaire se ridiculise et laisse la porte ouverte aux pseudo-sciences.

La sociologie, l'antithèse de Teissier

par ALAIN BOURDIN

La thèse de sociologie soutenue à l'université René-Descartes par l'astrologue Elizabeth Teissier n'est pas passée inaperçue, et provoque des réactions diverses. En première page d'un quotidien, les Prs Beaudelot et Establet s'indignent au nom de la rigueur sociologique («La .... une .... merce.»

L'on vient d'offrir à ceux que nous gênons un argument massif pour nous ridiculiser ou justifier l'appel aux pseudo-sociologues.
La sociologie – et la sociologie française reste l'une des .... ériliser, ...

giner l'avenir. Cette aventure dérisoire caricature un enjeu majeur: la reconquête de la sociologie par la société ●

Alain Bourdin *est professeur à l'Institut français d'urbanisme-université de Paris-VIII, laboratoire de théories des mutations urbaines, CNRS.*
.... ouvrage paru: «La Question locale», PUF, «La politique éclatée», 2000.

Figure 1.1   *The headline from Alain Bourdin's article in* Libération, *19 April 2001*

in the discipline's ability to bring about the better organization of society – or, as Bourdin put it, sociology's utility as 'an instrument for organising the present and imagining the future'.

In contrast, the following extract – also quoted by Hamilton and Thompson and taken from a newspaper article written by the British sociologist and broadcaster, Laurie Taylor – suggests a rather different emphasis:

> Back in the Seventies, it was difficult to find a sociologist working in the area of deviance who was not involved in participant observation. Academics could be found hanging out on street corners with youth gangs, sitting in squats with drug-users and standing on terraces with hooligans. A former colleague of mine remembers stepping off a late-night train at Waterloo and suddenly hearing a familiar voice issue from what looked like a bundle of old rags on a bench. 'Goodnight, Mary', said the voice. The bundle was an old friend from the University of Essex, pursuing research on vagrants.
>
> (*The Independent*, 8 June 2001, quoted in Hamilton and Thompson, 2002, p.x)

Whereas Bourdin and his interlocutors were preoccupied with issues of objectivity, the need to keep facts separate from values, and sociology's scientific credibility, the sociologists Taylor describes were clearly more concerned to get 'inside' the social worlds of the people they studied in order to *understand* these, as it were, through the eyes of the people themselves. Indeed, you may remember that this ambition informed a number of the studies you have previously come across in DD201 – for example, those of romance and the pub in *Understanding Everyday Life* (see **Redman, 2002; Watson, 2002**).

The differences evident in these two extracts point to a question lying at the heart of this chapter: what constitutes authoritative sociological knowledge? For example, is the authority of sociological knowledge best guaranteed by adopting a 'scientific' or 'objective' approach – perhaps one borrowed from the natural sciences (such as physics, chemistry and biology) – or are the objects of sociological enquiry rather different from those studied by natural scientists? If so, how might they best be studied? These questions are the subject of vigorous debate within sociology and have been answered in a number of competing ways. Needless to say, there is not space in the course of this chapter to explore the full range of these responses. However, the two positions on which we will be focusing – **'positivism'** and 'interpretivism' – are ones that have been central to the wider debate and, as such, provide a useful point of entry into it.

positivism

The chapter begins by introducing you to positivism. As you will discover, positivist sociologists seek to adopt (or adapt) the methods of the natural sciences and thereby study the social world in an 'objective' manner. However, in order to understand what it is that positivist sociologists admire in the scientific method, we need to understand what this method is (or, at least, what positivist sociologists understand it to be). In consequence, section 3 of the chapter investigates the scientific method – in particular, the experiment – as a basis for exploring how positivists have sought to apply this to the study of social phenomena. Section 4 then explores some of the challenges that arise in attempting to transfer the experimental method to the study of the social world – challenges that derive from the differences that exist between the objects of sociological enquiry and many of the objects studied by natural scientists. Positivism's robust responses to these challenges are investigated in the following section, while sections 6 and 7 explore a competing response: that provided by interpretivism. As these sections argue, for interpretivists, the nature of the social world demands a wholly different approach from that advocated by positivism. Section 8 summarizes the debate between positivism and interpretivism by drawing out some of the themes underlying the chapter's previous discussions. In particular, it focuses on *detachment* and *involvement* (should sociologists seek to remain detached from or be involved with their objects of study?); *explanation* and *understanding* (should sociologists seek to identify causal explanations in the manner of the natural scientist or to understand the meaningful character of local social worlds?); and *facts* and *values* (should sociologists only concern themselves with identifying facts or should they engage with moral and political issues as well?).

AIMS

The aims of this chapter are:

1   To introduce you to the debate about what constitutes authoritative knowledge about the social world.

2   To explore 'positivism' and 'interpretivism' as two important positions within this wider debate.

3   To investigate the precise nature of social phenomena as a basis for understanding why there is a debate about how they should be studied.

2   Positivist sociology

The introductory section to this chapter has already noted that, in studying the social world, positivist sociologists seek to adopt or adapt the criteria and methods of the natural sciences. Activity 1 explores this further and provides a brief overview of the history of positivist thought in the development of sociology.

ACTIVITY 1

Read and take notes from the extract below and then answer the following question:

What are the main features of the positivist approach to the study of social phenomena?

> The positivist approach – or positivism as it is also called – emerged from the historical influence of a growing and powerful eighteenth century philosophical movement known as the Enlightenment. This philosophy challenged the classical and religious ideas of an abstract 'higher authority', frequently religious, and the belief that problems could be solved purely by thinking. The Enlightenment provided the necessary intellectual climate for the emergence of sociology as the scientific study of society.
>
> What was particularly new about Enlightenment thinking was its assertion that reality could be observed and measured. Indeed, in one of its most powerful strands, it argued that 'true' knowledge derives from our senses: from the process of systematic observation and measurement. This new epistemology was (and still is) concerned with observable, measurable reality, using objective recording and categorization techniques. There was considerable emphasis on

mathematics, the establishment of universal laws of cause and effect and the exclusion of values and opinions.

In the nineteenth century, following achievements in the natural sciences, this scientific method came to be seen as one of the major means whereby problems in society should be examined. Auguste Comte, who is generally thought to be one of the founders of sociology, argued that society had become so complex that it could only be understood through observation, experience, and experimentation (Comte, 1971/1838). These are the basic principles of a 'scientific' approach. He wished to develop a discipline that could explain the social changes inherent in the shift from a society based largely on agriculture to one in which industry and capitalism were dominant. Later in the nineteenth century, Emile Durkheim used a similar approach in his efforts to have sociology recognized as the 'science' of society. He took the incidence of suicide as his research topic and used secondary data gathered from official records to argue that the relative breakdown of social cohesion in different social groups determined different suicide rates (Durkheim, 1951/1897). By the middle years of the twentieth century, this positivist view of what we can know and how we can know it was frequently taken for granted within sociology. It came increasingly under attack from the 1960s onwards but remains of great importance to this day.

Positivism, then, is an approach to social science which argues that social sciences should follow a 'natural' science model. It emphasizes the necessity for observation, measurement and the establishment of universal laws of cause and effect.

(adapted from Parr, 2002, pp.3–4)

As this extract makes clear, positivist sociology takes as its model a version of the scientific method. In particular, for positivist sociology, the authority of the natural sciences derives from:

- the direct *observation* and precise *measurement* of the phenomenon under study;
- the claimed ability of the scientist to remain *detached* from this object of study and thereby avoid confusing *facts* with *values*;
- and the ability to identify *causal explanations* that can serve as the basis for generating *universal laws*.

In this light, it will come as little surprise that, in *The Positive Philosophy*, the early positivist, Auguste Comte, famously identified 'social physics' (what we now call sociology) as one of the 'five fundamental sciences', the others being astronomy, physics, chemistry and physiology (Comte, 1971/1838, p.22).

But what exactly was this 'scientific method' the early positivists sought to borrow from the natural sciences and why was it that they saw in its techniques (observation, measurement, detachment and so forth) the means by which to guarantee the authority of their own research findings? In order to answer these questions, we need to investigate how the scientific method works.

Figure 1.2 *Auguste Comte (1798–1857), one of the founders of sociology and an early positivist*

SUMMARY OF SECTION 2

1 Positivism was influential in the establishment of sociology as a distinct discipline in the nineteenth century.

2 Positivist sociologists looked to the natural sciences for criteria and methods that would help guarantee the authority of sociological knowledge.

3 They stressed, in particular, the importance of: the direct observation and precise measurement of the phenomenon under study; the necessity of the sociologist remaining detached from this object of study, thereby avoiding confusing facts with values; and the significance of generating causal explanations that can serve as the basis for universal laws of social life.

3   Positivism and the experimental method in the natural sciences

As was noted at the end of the previous section, in order to understand exactly why the scientific method proved so attractive to early positivists working on sociological questions, we need to understand how this scientific method works – at least as understood within the positivist tradition. To pursue this, in the following activity you are going to explore an example of a scientific experiment of the sort that was influential on positivist thinking. The example – the French scientist Antoine Lavoisier's (1743–1794) famous 'mercury calx' experiment – is celebrated as the basis upon which the chemical element, oxygen, was first identified. (The following, together with sections 4 and 5, draws heavily on arguments developed by Mark J. Smith, 1998.)

ACTIVITY 2

Study the following description of Lavoisier's 'mercury calx' experiment. Try to focus on the basic principles that informed Lavoisier's use of an experimental method. In particular, ask yourself, in what way did Lavoisier seek to ensure that nothing outside the experiment interfered with the effects he observed?

> [In the eighteenth century], chemists were only beginning to understand gases, liquids and solids. … Antoine Lavoisier … used the experimental method to demonstrate the existence of a new gas, oxygen. … Lavoisier discovered that when sulphur or mercury was heated it formed a 'calx' (which was, in fact, a combination of the element with oxygen, forming an oxide). When the calx was, in turn, intensely heated within the enclosed space of the laboratory apparatus, the gas given off could be collected and subjected to investigation (as illustrated in [Figure 1.3 below]). It was discovered to be non-poisonous and to be flammable when kept in a pure state [that is, oxygen].
>
> (Smith, 1998, pp.38–9)

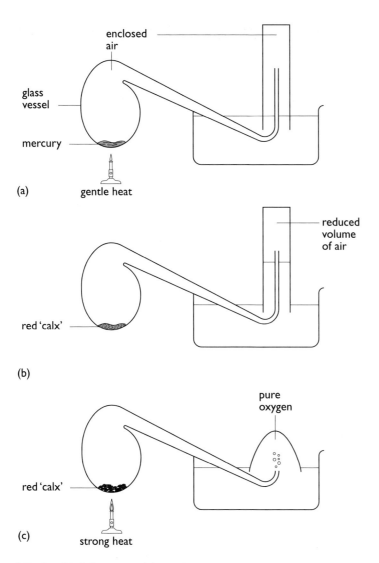

Figure 1.3   *Lavoisier's 'mercury calx' experiment*

As Figure 1.3 illustrates, Lavoisier's apparatus was designed to ensure a *closed system* in which the relationship between a limited number of entities (often called variables) could be observed without risk of interference from the outside. As you can see from Figure 1.3, the variables involved in the first stage of Lavoisier's experiment were mercury and air (or, strictly speaking, the air level) and, in the second stage, mercury oxide (the 'calx') and the air level. Limiting the number of variables within a closed system allowed him to identify with some certainty which change in which variable caused which outcome. In particular, he was able to show that heating mercury *causes* it to combine with something in the air to form a 'calx' (mercury oxide) and that heating mercury oxide *causes* it to release a gas in its pure form (subsequently identified as oxygen). Lavoisier was able to do this because the closed system design of his experiment ensured that no other variables were present to interfere with these events and nothing else changed in between them. In other words, because nothing else happened between, for instance, the heating of the mercury to form a 'calx' and the reduction in the volume of air in the test tube, and because nothing had interfered with this process, it was reasonable to conclude that the former led to the latter. (It is worth noting that, in descriptions of experiments like this, the variable that is manipulated by the researcher is usually called the experimental or *independent variable*, while the variable that changes as a result of this manipulation is called the *dependent variable*. In the first stage of Lavoisier's experiment the independent variable was the mercury and the dependent variable was the air level; in the second stage, the independent variable was the 'calx' and the dependent variable was again the air level.)

Having explored an actual example of a scientific experiment of the sort that influenced early positivists working on sociological questions, we are now in a better position to identify the exact principles they derived from this method. Perhaps most significantly, they identified *closed system analysis* (like that conducted by Lavoisier) as being central to the generation of authoritative knowledge. It was only by adopting (or adapting) this method, they argued, that sociological knowledge could be established as rigorous and authoritative ('true').

Similarly, early positivists also admired the experimental method's emphasis on *detached observation of objects*. For instance, Lavoisier could make a convincing case for his findings because he had *observed* the effects as they occurred. In short, his knowledge claim was based on observation of the object itself. This marked a break of revolutionary proportions from the past. Prior to the Enlightenment, the authority of knowledge had been based on received wisdom or established authority, such as that of the Church or the great thinkers of previous ages. With the advent of the experimental method, the authority of knowledge could – so positivists believed – be guaranteed by reference to objects themselves. In other words, for the early positivists, the experiment was seen as giving direct and unmediated knowledge of objects and thereby guaranteed that their descriptions of these were true.

Equally, the early positivists were impressed by the way in which closed system analysis appeared to ensure the separation of facts from values. For instance, because he observed the experiment from the outside – that is, because he remained *detached* from it – Lavoisier could make a convincing case that his findings were not influenced by his personal prejudices or preconceptions (that is, his values). This, so the early positivists thought, held out the promise of knowledge that was truly objective or value free.

Finally, early positivists saw in the experimental method the possibility of identifying 'universal laws' underlying social life. For example, because Lavoisier could successfully *repeat* his experiment, he was able to demonstrate that the effects he had observed were not a one-off or chance occurrence but stable features of the natural world (often referred to as 'empirical regularities'). For early positivists working on sociological questions this held out the possibility that they might also be able to identify 'empirical regularities': stable features of the social world that would allow them similarly to predict future outcomes with accuracy.

SUMMARY OF SECTION 3

1   The experimental method aims to produce causal explanations of observed phenomena. Its success in the natural sciences led positivists in the emergent field of sociology to look towards the experimental method as a model for their own research.

2   Positivists interpreted the experimental method as involving detached observation of a limited number of variables in a closed system such that facts are kept strictly separated from values.

3   By manipulating one (independent) variable within a closed system, and observing the effects of this manipulation on a second (dependent) variable, positivists argued that it can be reasonably concluded that there is a causal relationship between the variables (that the latter effect was caused by the former manipulation).

4   Where the outcome of such an experiment can be successfully repeated (and in the absence of other evidence 'falsifying' this result), positivists argue that it can be considered to be capable of successfully predicting future outcomes and thus to have the status of a 'scientific law'.

5   This approach grounds knowledge claims in the observation of objects (as opposed to received wisdom or established authority). In their attempt to borrow this approach and apply it to the study of the social world, early positivists sought to address social phenomena as objects that could be detached from the person studying them.

4   The challenge of applying the experimental method to the study of the social world

Although early positivists working on social questions saw in the experimental method a model for generating authoritative knowledge, transferring this method to the study of the social world presented a number of challenges. In particular:

■   the *subject–object problem*;
■   the difficulty of achieving *experimental closure* when studying social phenomena; and,
■   the difficulty of achieving *ecological validity*.

Let's explore each of these in turn.

4.1   The subject–object problem in sociological research

When Antoine Lavoisier conducted his mercury calx experiment, it was reasonable for him to assume that the mercury he used was a separate entity, not easily confused with his own person. This made the task of keeping his values (for instance, his personal beliefs, preconceptions, and the social conventions of his day) separate from his observations relatively uncomplicated.

This task is inherently more complex for the sociological researcher who is inevitably part of the social world she or he studies. For instance, when Diane Watson studied pubs (as explored in Chapter 5 of *Understanding Everyday Life*, see **Watson, 2002**), she could not simply stand outside or detach herself from the cultural meanings that pubs have in the contemporary UK because she was herself part of the social world in which these meanings are generated. This does not mean that her research was hopelessly 'biased', nor, for that matter, does it mean that natural scientific research, like Lavoisier's, is necessarily value free. What it does mean, however, is that compared with the natural scientist the sociological researcher cannot so easily adopt the position of the 'detached observer'. In short, the subject of sociological research (the researcher) is intimately interrelated with the objects she or he studies (hence, the 'subject–object problem').

To make matters more complicated still, many of the objects of social research are inherently 'fuzzy', which is to say they are subjective and contingent (Yates, 2004, pp.21–2). For instance, imagine a sociological researcher wanted to identify the factors influencing alcohol consumption. One question he might ask is 'what makes a drink pleasurable?' (on the assumption that, if it is pleasurable to drink something, people are more likely to do so). Needless to say, as well as being of interest to sociologists of everyday life concerned to identify the meanings people attach to their social worlds, the answer to this question would also be of considerable interest to the manufacturers of alcohol and, from a different perspective, health providers (indeed, you will come across an example of social research conducted by a drinks manufacturer in the audio-visual material associated with this module). The challenge for the sociological researcher is that 'pleasure' is not easily made into an objective entity and, unlike a chemical element, cannot be simply observed from the 'outside'. Instead, pleasure is a complex social phenomenon made up of diverse preferences and cultural meanings. In Chapter 5 of *Understanding Everyday Life*, Diane Watson underlined this point, arguing that, particularly in the contemporary consumer cultures characteristic of the advanced industrialized economies of the West, it is important to recognize that:

> … consumption is both a material and a symbolic activity, expressive of identities, lifestyles and taste … when individuals enter a particular pub they are purchasing far more than a material product, such as a drink … They are also purchasing an experience or ambience, which is associated with desire, and the creation and expression of identity and lifestyle. What is important is not so much the actual products that are consumed but the meanings attached to those products.
>
> **(Watson, 2002, p.207)**

Bourdieu
habitus

As this suggests, what makes a drink 'pleasurable' cannot be separated from what **Bourdieu** referred to as a person's **'habitus'** – that is, the ingrained values, dispositions, habits, modes of classification and so forth that structure people's experience of the world around them and which they often simply take for granted (see **Savage, 2002, pp.76–82**). Depending on their habitus, a drink that is for one person profoundly enjoyable will, for someone else, be too 'masculine' or too 'feminine'; too 'childlike' or too 'grown-up'; too 'posh' or too 'common', and so on. In describing a social phenomenon like pleasure as 'fuzzy' we are, then, pointing to the fact that standing 'outside' and observing it in a detached manner as if it were an objective entity or 'thing' is not as simple or straightforward as it often appears to be for natural scientists.

This argument also applies to social phenomena that might, at first glance, appear to possess more obviously material dimensions. For instance, the family might be thought of as an objective entity that can be easily observed in a detached manner. After all, unlike an emotion such as a pleasure, it has a distinct material existence (individual family members and their activities). However, as you saw in Reading 1.1 of *Understanding Everyday Life*, the form family life has taken has changed quite dramatically over time and varies according to such factors as class and ethnicity (see **Hareven, 1993**). Families, it would seem, are not objective entities, given in nature, but are social phenomena that are made and remade by people via their collective activities and the meanings they attribute to these. In short, while it is relatively easy to stand 'outside' an object such as a chemical element, this is more complicated in the case of a social phenomenon such as the family because, unlike a chemical element, what we call 'the family' does not exist separately from the changing social meanings and activities that constitute it.

4.2   The difficulty of achieving experimental closure

The second challenge facing the sociologist attempting to transfer the experimental method to the study of social phenomena concerns the difficulty of achieving levels of closure comparable to those possible in the natural sciences (although we should note that closure can also be difficult to achieve in the natural sciences). One of the most obvious reasons for this is ethical. In many instances, it would be simply unacceptable to perform closed experiments on people because they would be likely to have an adverse effect on their well-being. However, there is also another issue: the fact that, unlike many of the objects of natural scientific enquiry, people change.

For instance, Lavoisier could take for granted the fact that the variables he was studying (mercury and air) were the same each time he conducted his experiment. As a result, he could reasonably conclude that, because the variables had not changed, the effect he observed (the formation of mercury oxide and the release of oxygen when this was heated) was the same in each case. Sociologists, however, do not have this advantage. Because they study people and the social worlds they construct, they have to take into account the likelihood that their object of study will change over time and from context to context. In particular, as we have previously noted, people will give different *meanings* to their actions according to the precise cultural world or habitus in which they live.

Imagine, for instance, that we devised an experiment to test whether or not drinking a particular wine 'causes pleasure' (leaving aside for now the issue of how to define and observe a fuzzy concept such as 'pleasure'). We might isolate a participant in a bare room (to ensure that any pleasure observed was not the result of external factors such as the presence of friends or the ambience created deliberately by a bar owner); let her drink a particular wine; and then ask her to record whether or not this was pleasurable. Although the results from this experiment might have use (after all, this procedure is not dissimilar from that adopted by professional wine-tasters), they could not be expected to have the same kind of *authority* as those produced by Lavoisier. In particular, in attempting to replicate our findings we could not be sure that we would be observing exactly the same phenomenon in each case. For instance, if we repeated the experiment with the same participant over a number of years only to find that she no longer liked the wine, would this mean that our original finding was wrong, or could it be that her taste had changed as a consequence of increased age, or that she had simply changed her mind? Similarly, if we repeated the experiment with different participants only to find that they too did not like the wine, would this necessarily tell us anything about the wine or might it simply reflect a difference in habitus? In other words, would differing preferences indicate the tastes characteristic of, for instance, different social classes rather than telling us anything 'objective' about the wine itself?

As this example begins to illustrate, because social phenomena (like the experience of 'pleasure') are not objective entities or 'things' equivalent to those studied in the natural sciences but are, instead, inextricably bound up with values and meanings, they cannot reasonably be assumed to be the same over time and in all contexts. As you will see in the next section, this does not preclude the possibility of studying social phenomena as objects and in a detached manner, but it does mean that it is often difficult for sociologists to achieve the same degree of experimental closure that is possible in the natural sciences. An important consequence of this is that it is also often difficult for sociologists to identify causal relationships capable of predicting future outcomes with any degree of certainty. Needless to say, this limits sociology's ability to generate universal laws comparable to those in the natural sciences.

4.3   Ecological validity

The third factor that makes transferring the experimental method to the study of the social world challenging concerns what is often called 'ecological validity'. This refers to the difficulty of transferring results generated from observation of a limited number of variables in a closed system to the open systems that characterize the social world. We can illustrate this by returning once more to our example of what makes a drink pleasurable. Even if we could design an experiment that successfully identified a causal relationship between consumption of a specific drink and the experience of pleasure, we could not guarantee that this result would be replicated in the 'real' world of social interactions. For instance, look again at the following extract from Ann Whitehead's study of pub cultures in rural Herefordshire (taken from Reading 5.3 in Chapter 5 of *Understanding Everyday Life*):

> In the pub men were brought together into focused interaction … in a situation of defined equality in which drinking sustained and made possible a whole set of other activities. … Within the pub, activity might be focused on darts, or quoits or on a card game, but the primary activity was verbal. … Frequently, … the conversation developed into a highly characteristic set of exchanges in which joking and humour were uppermost. …
>
> … The dynamic of the exchange involved finding a point of vulnerability in another customer … and pointing to it by a remark which made everyone laugh. …
>
> [Often] [t]he major content of teasing of this kind was the degree of control that a married man exerted over his wife's behaviour. … Rows and quarrels in which he had the upper hand brought a man esteem, but if his wife rowed with him, locked him out of the house or refused to cook for him, he lost esteem.
>
> **(Whitehead, 1976, pp.223–4)**

As this suggests, drinkers at The Wagonner certainly experienced pleasure but much of this was to do with the competitive 'banter' that characterized interactions in the bar rather than drinking itself. More significantly, whether or not the banter proved pleasurable depended, in part, on an individual's skill in holding his own in a given interaction and, in part, on his success in hiding anything (such as 'not being able to control his wife') that might make him a target of banter. In other words, whether or not a drink in The Wagonner was pleasurable depended on a multiplicity of factors that combined together in a manner often difficult to predict in advance and that changed over time and from one context to another. As you will probably recognize, the multiplicity of factors in play in any given interaction in The Wagonner means that, even if we had established that in an experimental setting a Wagonner 'regular' found the consumption of a particular drink pleasurable, there is no guarantee that this result would be repeated in the real life setting of the pub. In short, experimental results often have 'low ecological validity' when applied to everyday social life.

SUMMARY OF SECTION 4

1   The subject–object problem means that, compared with the natural scientist, the social researcher cannot as easily stand 'outside' the object of her or his research and observe it in a detached manner.

2   It is often more difficult to achieve experimental closure in sociology than in the natural sciences because, unlike many of the objects of natural scientific enquiry, those studied by sociologists are often not stable or constant.

3   Findings from closed system experiments often have low 'ecological validity' – that is, they are often difficult to translate to the complex and changing conditions of the social world.

5   Positivist responses to the complexity of the social world

In the preceding sections we have explored the criteria and methods positivist sociologists identified as being central to the natural sciences and examined some of the challenges they faced in trying to transfer these to the rather different conditions of the social world. However, as was noted above, the fact that, in comparison with the natural sciences, it is often difficult to study social phenomena as objects does not mean that this is impossible. In this section, we will be investigating exactly how positivist sociologists have adapted the scientific method to the study of the social world. This will involve exploration of aspects of quantitative research methods. You will go on to explore these in greater detail in Chapter 3 of this book. However, our immediate interest lies in how positivist sociologists have sought to use them to adapt the underlying logic of experimentation to the study of social phenomena.

5.1   Adapting the experimental method

One of the most obvious responses positivist sociologists have made to the challenge of transferring the experimental method to the social world has been to *adapt* this method better to address the conditions of this world. In particular, positivist sociologists (in common with other social scientists) have adopted the logic of *comparison* in conducting experiments and/or have undertaken experiments 'in the field' as opposed to in the laboratory. The latter response – the use of field experiments – involves applying the experimental method in 'real life' conditions. As such, it seeks to address the problem of ecological validity. The former response – the logic of comparison – addresses the difficulty, identified in the previous section, of achieving experimental closure when studying social phenomena. You will probably remember that this difficulty arises because, unlike chemical elements, the objects of sociological enquiry (people) cannot reasonably be assumed to be constant and stable. To address this, sociological (and other) researchers often divide their participants into two groups: an experimental group (the subject of the intervention) and a second 'control' or comparison group who are not subject to any intervention. If an effect is observed in the first, experimental group (the one subject to the intervention) but not in the control group, researchers can make a more authoritative claim that this effect has been caused by the intervention and not by some other factor of which they were unaware.

To illustrate these points, we can consider a famous example where both methods were used (for a fuller discussion, see Sapsford, 1996, pp.127–8). During the 1950s, in response to rising levels of road traffic fatalities, the Governor of Connecticut in the United States ordered a police and judicial 'crackdown' on motorists caught speeding. The following year, there was a 12 per cent fall in road accident fatalities. One obvious reading of this fall would be to interpret it as a consequence of or caused by the Governor's intervention. However, since this intervention was made in an open system rather than a closed system like that pertaining in an experiment, any number of other variables could also have been at work. For example, Connecticut motorists may have been responding to increased coverage of road traffic fatalities in the national media, or weather conditions might have been better that year leading to fewer fatal accidents.

A decade or so later, a group of researchers decided to test whether or not the Governor's intervention was the causal factor behind the 12 per cent fall in road accident fatalities (Campbell and Ross, 1968). To do this, they compared the Connecticut figures with equivalent statistics from a 'control' group of four other states where a crackdown had not been implemented. This revealed that the drop in road accident fatalities was sharper in Connecticut than elsewhere, suggesting that the Governor's intervention had indeed had some impact on these figures. This illustrates how the logic of experimentation can be adapted to sociological research in order to address both the issue of ecological validity and the problem of achieving levels of experimental closure comparable to those often possible in the natural sciences.

5.2   Constructing measures

Although sociological positivists have adapted the experimental method to the social world, this method has been used more systematically in social psychology. More common in sociology has been the use of social surveys (these will be explored in more detail in Chapter 3 of this volume). Surveys involve gathering quantitative information (information that can be presented in numerical form) from a selection of people from a larger population, carefully chosen to ensure their characteristics match those of this larger population (a 'representative sample'). This necessitates asking people questions that can be answered in a simple 'tick box' or 'yes/no' fashion which in turn means that the questions have to be carefully calibrated to ensure that they capture the major dimensions of the concept under study. This involves 'operationalizing' the concept in the form of a 'measure' and is particularly important where the concept under study is 'fuzzy'. (As you will recall, this refers to the fact that the objects of sociological enquiry – for example, the concept of 'pleasure' – often mean different things to different people and are subject to change.)

Figure 1.4 shows an example of such a measure, the Leeds Dependency Questionnaire (LDQ) (Raistrick *et al.*, 1994), designed to operationalize the concept of 'alcohol dependence'.

In answering the questions please:

Think about the last week.

Tick the answer that's most appropriate to you.

	Never code as 0	Sometimes code as 1	Often code as 2	Nearly always code as 3
Do you find yourself thinking about when you will next be able to have another drink?				
Is drinking more important than anything else you might do during the day?				
Do you feel your need for drink is too strong to control?				
Do you plan your days around getting and taking a drink?				
Do you drink in a particular way in order to increase the effect it gives you?				
Do you drink morning, afternoon and evening?				
Do you feel you have to carry on drinking once you have started?				
Is getting the effect you want more important than the particular drink or drug you use?				
Do you want to take more drink when the effect starts to wear off?				
Do you find it difficult to cope with life without drink?				

Figure 1.4 *The Leeds Dependency Questionnaire operationalizes a 'fuzzy' social phenomenon: alcohol dependence*
Source of data: Raistrick *et al.*, 1994

As you can see from Figure 1.4, not only does this measure seek to capture the major dimensions of a 'fuzzy' phenomenon, one to which people will give different meanings, it also allows researchers to assign a numerical value (from 0 to 3) to individual responses. For instance, because the measure has 10 questions, a person who answered 'never' to each of these questions would receive a score of zero (since each 'never' answer is assigned a value of zero), while a person who answered 'nearly always' to each would receive a score of 30 (since each answer of this kind is assigned a value of three). As this illustrates, despite the fact that alcohol dependence is a fuzzy concept, it can be rendered into a form that is susceptible to measurement – that is, it can be treated like an object. A person who receives a score approaching zero will be judged to have a low level of alcohol dependence, while a person with a score approaching 30 will be judged to have a high level.

5.3   Establishing relationships between variables via statistical analyses

Although the operationalization of concepts allows for the measurement of social phenomena, such measurement is only the first step towards identifying relationships between variables. You will recall that the point of an experiment is to establish the presence or absence of relationships between the variables under study and that the scientist does this by manipulating one variable to see if this causes an effect on the others in the experiment. Obviously, in a social survey this is not possible, so how does a sociologist seek to identify such relationships?

Take a look at Table 1.1. This provides a hypothetical and very simplified version of data that might be generated from a survey. As you can see, the data provide numerical information on respondents' ages and the number of units of alcohol they consume in a given week.

Table 1.1   A simplified illustration of a table comparing age with units of alcohol consumed in a week

	Age (in years)	Units of alcohol consumed in a week
Respondent 1	20	5
Respondent 2	30	10
Respondent 3	40	15
Respondent 4	50	20
Respondent 5	60	25

A glance at the hypothetical evidence provided by Table 1.1 suggests that, as age increases, alcohol consumption also increases. This is what is called a 'positive correlation' (meaning that the variables – age and units of alcohol consumed – go in the same direction, in this case up). If the variables went in opposite directions (that is, as age increased, alcohol consumption decreased), this would be called a 'negative correlation'. Alternatively, the figures might reveal no pattern at all, indicating the absence of any correlation between alcohol consumption and increasing age. However, if – as in this case – a positive or negative correlation is present, it can be taken to suggest that the variables may be related in some way.

Needless to say, the numerical data with which sociologists work are rarely as obvious or simple as those used in Table 1.1. In consequence, they would usually have to identify the extent of a relationship between variables using statistical tests, today often done by computer. However, you will need to remember that, even where a statistical test has demonstrated a possible relationship between two variables, this does not indicate that one variable *causes* the other. For instance, in the case of Table 1.1, it is clear that an increase in the respondents' alcohol consumption will not have caused them to grow older (they would have done so anyway). However, this does not mean that we can conclude that increased age will have *caused* the respondents increased alcohol consumption. While it might be the case that, for example, being older makes one more likely to drink because one is more likely to be tolerant of alcohol, an alternative and equally valid hypothesis might be that it is a *third* and unknown variable that has caused the relationship. For instance, it could be that, as people get older, they are likely to earn more money and therefore spend more on alcohol. In order to reach a final decision about the existence of a causal relationship between increasing age and alcohol consumption we would, then, need to carry out much more research.

As this example illustrates, statistical analyses mean that positivist sociologists have not been restricted to the use of the experimental method in seeking to establish significant relationships between variables. In particular, statistical analyses allow sociological researchers to 'control' (or exclude) variables that are irrelevant or less significant in producing a particular effect and to identify with some degree of authority the extent to which variables are likely to be related to each other.

Common to all the procedures we have explored in section 5 – the use of control groups; field experiments; the careful operationalization of concepts; and statistical analyses – is an attempt to adapt the underlying logic of experimentation to the complexity of the social world and thereby to apply positivist criteria for generating authoritative knowledge to the study of this. In particular, in applying these procedures, positivist sociologists argue that they are able:

- to study social phenomena as objects;
- to observe and measure these in a detached manner using closed system analysis;
- to keep facts and values separate; and,
- to identify causal explanations as a basis for accurately predicting future outcomes.

However, it is important to note that not everyone who adopts such procedures will identify themselves as a positivist. Indeed, as the next section will argue (and as you will go on to explore in Chapter 3 of this volume), some 'lighter' versions of interpretivism also use quantitative methods. In other words, it is quite possible to use quantitative methods without assuming they ensure the separation of facts from values, the objective status of social phenomena and so forth.

SUMMARY OF SECTION 5

1　Positivist sociologists have developed a number of robust responses to the challenges posed in applying the experimental method to the social world.

2　These include: adapting the experimental method itself; the careful operationalization of concepts to address the often 'fuzzy' nature of social phenomena; and the use of social surveys and statistical analyses to identify possible relationships between variables.

3　In adapting the underlying logic of the experimental method to the study of social phenomena, positivist sociologists have continued to emphasize the following criteria for generating authoritative knowledge: the importance of treating social phenomena as objects; detached observation and measurement; the use of closed system analyses; the separation of facts from values; and the identification of causal explanations as a basis for accurately predicting future outcomes.

4　It is important to remember that not everyone who uses quantitative methods will adhere to positivist criteria for generating authoritative knowledge.

6　Searching for the actor's point of view: the interpretivist tradition

Although it is possible to argue that positivist sociologists have developed successful procedures for applying the logic of experimentation to the study of the social world, it is also possible to argue that the specific character of social phenomena demands a wholly different approach to the generation of authoritative knowledge. This position has been developed, in particular, within a tradition of sociological thought often referred to as 'interpretivism'. Activity 3 provides an introduction to the main principles underlying the interpretivist approach, together with a brief overview of its historical development.

ACTIVITY 3

Read and take notes from the following description of interpretivism and then answer the following questions:

1　What are the main features of the interpretivist tradition to the study of social phenomena?

2　How do these differ from positivism?

The interpretivist tradition is generally considered to have entered sociology via the work of Max Weber (1864–1920) and the wider *Methodenstreit* ('dispute about method') that began in the late nineteenth century. In contrast to the positivist position, a number of commentators involved in the *Methodenstreit* argued that the study of the social world demands procedures fundamentally different from those adopted in the natural sciences. Whereas the latter are concerned with identifying causal explanations and generating universal laws, the social sciences, they argued, should be concerned with *understanding* (*Verstehen*): in particular, understanding what is unique, specific or particular in human conduct and affairs (Outhwaite, 2000). In Weber's work, this wider argument took the form of an emphasis on meaningful human activity (see, for example, Weber, 1968/1922).

Although he continued to be sympathetic to aspects of the positivist project, Weber was one of the first sociologists to argue that it was not possible to discover universal laws of human behaviour based on the same research methods as those used in the natural sciences. This, he argued, was because the object of sociological research is human activity and, in order to understand this, one must look at the meanings that people attribute to their actions. In other words, for Weber, we can only understand human activity by seeing it from the actor's perspective. Weber's '*verstehende* sociology' was, then, one that focused on understanding the way in which people make sense of, or interpret, their collective activities and, in the process, create their social worlds. As such, it laid the foundation for a critique of positivism and the development of an alternative interpretive tradition.

Although drawing on slightly different roots, an interpretivist tradition also flourished during the years between the First and Second World Wars in the work of the **Chicago School**. The Chicago School is perhaps most famous for developing **symbolic interactionism**, a 'stronger' version of interpretivism than that made available by Weber (see, for example, Mead, 1934). Although much of its work involved the continued use of social surveys and statistical analysis, the Chicago School is also justly famous for its ground-breaking studies utilizing detailed case histories of individual lives and ethnographic observation and description (for two iconic Chicago texts, see William Isaac Thomas and Florian Znaniecki's (1918/19/20) *The Polish Peasant in Europe and America* and Clifford Shaw's (1930) *The Jack-Roller: A Delinquent Boy's Own Story*).

Chicago School symbolic interactionism

During the middle years of the twentieth century, the interpretivist tradition, both in the United States and Europe, was largely submerged by positivism. However, beginning slowly in late 1950s and with increasing rapidity from the 1970s, the positivist tide began to retreat, such that, by the 1980s, even 'strong' interpretivist approaches had become part of the mainstream of sociological enquiry. This resurgence was fuelled, in particular, by feminist and other politically radical researchers critical of positivism's claims to scientific 'objectivity'. These researchers argued that, far from being objective, positivist sociology had merely served to obscure women's and other marginalized social groups' experience of subordination. For such researchers, interpretivist approaches held out the possibility of better understanding the lives of marginalized social groups and thereby challenging their oppressed positions.

In sum, the aim of interpretive sociology is to 'understand the complex world of lived experience from the point of view of those who live in it' (Denzin and Lincoln, 1994, p.118). Whereas positivism seeks to observe, measure and explain human activity, as it were, from the 'outside', interpretivist approaches seek to *understand* it from the 'inside' – that is, 'starting from the actor's point of view' (Bryman, 1988, p.24).

(adapted from Parr, 2002, pp.6–7)

What does Activity 3 tell us about the interpretivist tradition and its relationship to positivism? Clearly, the starting point of the interpretivist approach is the claim that the objects of sociological enquiry – that is, people and their collective forms of life – are fundamentally different from those found in the natural sciences and therefore demand different criteria and methods for generating authoritative knowledge. This is because, so interpretivists argue, unlike the objects of natural scientific enquiry, which can reasonably be considered to be objective entities (stable features of the natural world that are separate from the researcher), the things that sociologists study are the outcome of *meaningful social activity*. For instance, as was argued in section 4.1, the pleasure to be derived from a particular drink is inextricably bound up with a person's habitus and is thus shaped by a rich and complex array of social conventions, classificatory practices and rules of conduct. As this makes clear, the pleasure experienced in relation to drinking is not simply a feature of nature (although we obviously need fluids to survive). Rather, it is made and remade by people in their ongoing interactions.

Positivist sociologists are, of course, not unaware of the distinction between the objects of natural scientific and sociological enquiry, a fact that has informed the various means by which they have sought to adapt the logic of experimentation to the complexities of the social world (see section 5 above). However, for interpretivists, these attempts seldom go far enough. For instance, interpretivists argue that, although positivist sociologists pay careful attention to operationalizing concepts (as we saw in the Leeds Dependency Questionnaire in section 5.2 above), the measures they construct are often insufficiently sensitive to capture the specific nuances of social meaning fabricated in a particular locality and interaction. As a result, so interpretivists argue, the responses people make to such questionnaires often fail to reflect the social meanings they themselves give to their activities and instead reflect the values and meanings contained in the questionnaire. In other words, rather than eliciting the specific values and meanings active in a particular social site or interaction, measures of the sort used by positivist sociologists risk *imposing* the researchers' own values and meanings on to these.

A particularly powerful example of this is to be found in Hollway and Jefferson's (2000, pp.7–25) critique of 'fear of crime' surveys. These, they argue, tend to ask a question such as 'How safe do you feel walking alone in this area after dark?' and then assume that people's responses to this can be measured as if they are the same thing and as if that thing is an objective entity whose meanings are constant across time and different social contexts. As Hollway and Jefferson argue, these assumptions are almost certainly spurious. For example, the possible threat posed by 'walking alone in the dark' is likely to be different for different social groups: for men the threat might arise from the risk of getting into a fight; for women, it might be sexual assault. Because the responses given to it will not necessarily refer to the same threat, this means that the question will not be measuring the same thing each time it is asked. Worse still, it is not clear whether people's responses to the question will actually reflect their fear of crime or some other fear. Hollway and Jefferson argue that the question is just as likely to generate a more general or irrational anxiety conjured up by the image of walking alone on a dark night – in other words, 'the stuff of horror fiction … and nightmares' (Hollway and Jefferson, 2000, p.9). In short, fear of crime surveys assume they are measuring something objective but it is not at all clear this is the case. Values, it would seem, have crept in via the back door.

In a similar vein, many 'strong' interpretivists argue that, because social phenomena (like the example of pub 'banter' discussed in section 4.3 above) occur in open systems and are, therefore, the outcome of complex and multiple factors that combine in unpredictable ways, searching for causal relationships that can serve as the basis for predicting future outcomes is a largely fruitless exercise. Instead, they suggest, we should concentrate on understanding what is particular to and specific about the social phenomenon under study.

In a moment, we will go on to explore the implications of these arguments through a worked example. However, before doing this, a word of caution is in order. The example we will investigate, in common with many interpretivist studies, utilizes qualitative research methods (explored in more detail in Chapter 2 of this volume). Qualitative methods are often preferred by interpretivist sociologists because they promise to give access to what is specific and local to particular social worlds. In other words, they promise to give access to the 'actor's point of view'. However, we should not make the mistake of assuming that adopting an interpretivist position necessitates the use of qualitative methods (or, for that matter, that positivists will wholly eschew the use of qualitative data). This is because, as Activity 3 hints, some versions of interpretivism (particularly those associated with the work of Weber) remain sympathetic to aspects of positivist thought. Although Weber believed in 'starting from the actor's point of view' (thus rejecting the notion of social phenomena as objectively existing entities equivalent to those found in the natural sciences), he retained a commitment, if in modified form, to explanation, prediction and objectivity in sociological research. As a result, studies influenced by Weber's approach use many of the same quantitative research methods as those often adopted by positivists – in particular, the social survey (for a famous example, see Rex and Moore, 1967). The exact details of Weber's argument need not detain us here. The point to grasp is that interpretivism is a broad church containing stronger and 'lighter' (that is, weaker) approaches. These 'lighter' forms of interpretivism are as likely to use quantitative as they are qualitative methods (you will want to keep this in mind when studying quantitative methods in Chapter 3 of this volume).

SUMMARY OF SECTION 6

1   Interpretivists argue that, since the objects of sociological enquiry are fundamentally different from those found in the natural sciences, the criteria and methods for generating authoritative knowledge adopted in the natural sciences are inappropriate for sociological study.

2   Interpretivist approaches start from the position that social phenomena are made and remade as part of meaningful social activity. In consequence, they argue that generating authoritative sociological knowledge involves getting 'inside' the particular social world in question and understanding it 'through the eyes' of those whose social activities constitute that world.

3   Interpretivism contains stronger and 'lighter' versions. Lighter versions, in particular, often use quantitative as well as qualitative methods.

7 Exploring interpretivism

In Activity 3, the extract you studied concluded by saying that interpretivist sociology seeks to '*understand* [the social world] from the "inside" – that is, "starting from the actor's point of view"'. The aim of what follows is to use a worked example to explore exactly what this means. This will involve returning to a reading you first came across in Chapter 5 of *Understanding Everyday Life*, 'Learning the ropes in a dipsomaniac's paradise' by Diane Watson **(Watson, 2001)** (reproduced as Reading 1.1 at the end of this chapter). As Watson explained in her original discussion of this reading, the material comes from fieldnotes she compiled while undertaking participant observation of bar work as part of an ethnographic study of a small business enterprise. These methods were discussed briefly in Chapter 5 of *Understanding Everyday Life* and will be explored in more detail in Chapter 2 of this book. However, in this section, we are less concerned with the methods themselves than with the 'strong' version of interpretivism they represent – one that has its roots in the ethnographic studies conducted by the Chicago School in the 1920s and 1930s (for an overview of the history of ethnographic research in twentieth-century sociology, see **Bennett and Watson, 2002b, pp.xvi–xvii**).

READING 1.1

You should now read 'Learning the ropes in a dipsomaniac's paradise', by Diane Watson, which is reproduced as Reading 1.1. As you may remember, the study from which these fieldnotes are taken aimed to understand bar work from the 'inside'. As you read, think about the following questions:

1   What social conventions and practices constituted bar work in this particular pub?

2   What does it mean to say that bar work is a 'meaningful social activity'?

3   Were there particular meanings or practices that were specific to the pub (that is, that would be unlikely to be found in all pubs)?

4   How possible would it be to use Watson's research to make predictions about future outcomes, whether related to bar work in this particular pub or others?

5   In studying bar work, why might it be useful to begin 'from the actor's point of view'?

Watson's fieldnotes clearly provide a vivid description of what it feels like to start a new job with barely adequate training. However, as they are intended to do, they also tell us much about the meanings, practices and conventions that constitute bar work. For instance, one of the most obvious features of the account is its emphasis on the range of technical competencies or practices that bar work involves: pulling pints; using optics; memorising the prices of drinks; adding up rounds; taking and submitting food orders, and so on. Similarly, the account underlines the extent to which these practices are embedded in social conventions or informal rules of conduct that not only structure the social interactions of bar work, particularly those with customers, but also carry social meaning. For example, the author was told that she should always serve customers before washing glasses and should endeavour to catch the eye of customers queuing to be served so that they would be aware they were next in line. These are examples of informal bar work conventions that are, in part, designed to convey to customers the meaning that they are valued (serving the customer is more important than washing glasses) and that their attempt to queue will be reciprocated.

The fact that Watson had to be taught many of these informal rules of conduct (or discover them through trial and error) indicates their profoundly social character. They are not simply instinctual or individual but made, negotiated and remade by bar workers and their customers as they interact with each other. A good example of this is to be found in Watson's description of the incident with the romantically involved couple who ordered a Martini and lemonade. As Watson explains, her inability to use the Martini optic contravened a cardinal but still tacit rule underlying bar workers' interactions with customers: that the bar tender's entitlement to be in charge of the interaction is dependent on her maintaining an air of competence. Watson's all too evident incompetence allowed the customer to

Figure 1.5 *Diane Watson getting an 'insider's view' of bar work*

renegotiate this tacit rule and to start making demands that he would otherwise not have made. Needless to say, this incident shares many similarities with Garfinkel's 'breaching experiments' described in Chapter 3 of *Understanding Everyday Life* (see **Hamilton, 2002a, pp.99–100**). As Hamilton explains, Garfinkel set out deliberately to break the tacit rules governing everyday interactions in order to expose their existence. Watson's contravention of the rule that bar workers should appear competent was, of course, inadvertent. Nevertheless, in allowing the customer to renegotiate the terms of the convention, it served to bring its existence into the open.

The convention described in this incident – that the bar tender is in charge of the interaction involved in purchasing a drink – is, of course, not one that is particular to the pub in which Diane Watson did her fieldwork. Indeed, it is common to retail work generally. As this suggests, many of the meanings, practices and conventions in operation in a given interaction or local site will draw on a wider repertoire of what is considered socially normal and appropriate. However, as Watson's fieldnotes indicate, there is considerable local variation in these meanings, practices and conventions. An obvious example was the discount offered to employees of the theatre to which the pub was attached, a discount that represented a local variation in the rules of conduct surrounding the purchasing of a drink. A more interesting example is suggested by Watson's passing reference to the 'silly drinks' kept in the cabinets behind the bar. Although it is possible to read this as merely reflecting Watson's own views of these drinks, the use of inverted commas suggests that the phrase was one common to the bar workers in this particular pub (or, perhaps, pubs like it). This implies that the bar workers attributed a hierarchy of value to the drinks they sold, one in which the 'odd concoctions' found in the cabinets were positioned as inherently less 'serious' than some other drinks – for example, the 'real' ale sold from hand pumps at the bar. It seems likely that this hierarchy of value is one that, if not specific to this particular pub, is at least restricted to pubs having a similar ethos. For instance, other retailers might well consider real ale to be 'boring' or 'middle-aged' and the so-called 'silly drinks' to be 'youthful' and 'fun'.

This interplay between a wider social repertoire of meanings, practices and conventions in bar work and local variations of these begins to suggest some important issues related to the 'generalizability' of Watson's findings – that is, the extent to which they can be applied to bar work in other contexts or used as the basis to predict future outcomes. You will remember that one of the ambitions of positivist sociology is to identify significant relationships between key variables (for example, age and alcohol consumption) as a basis for generating causal explanations capable of making accurate predictions. It is clear that Watson's fieldnotes do not provide information of this kind. Rather than focusing on two or three key variables, they offer a description of what bar work feels like and a detailed exploration of one person's experience in a particular pub. In fact, interpretivist sociologists are often uninterested in generalizing from their findings, focusing instead on what is local and particular to the social phenomenon they are studying. For interpretivist sociologists of this kind, social phenomena are inherently fragile and transitory because made and remade in social interaction. However, other interpretivists argue that, because the meanings, practices and conventions active in local social worlds often draw on wider social repertoires and are informed by wider social relations (as was the case in Watson's study), it is often possible to draw more general conclusions from interpretivist research.

For example, in the case of Diane Watson's fieldnotes, it might be possible to generate a model of the learning process that an inexperienced bar tender needs to go through before she or he becomes fully competent. This could then be tested in other pubs and modified until it addressed the widest possible range of conditions while still remaining a coherent model. A model of this kind would prove valuable in, for instance, improving staff training. However, we would need to remember that it could not be used to predict a specific outcome with any accuracy (for instance, how long a particular trainee bar worker would take to become competent) and would not have the status of a scientific law equivalent to those generated in the natural sciences.

All of this begins to suggest why interpretivist sociologists consider it so important to 'begin from the actor's point of view'. If Diane Watson had not undertaken participant observation in an attempt to understand bar work 'through the eyes' of an inexperienced bar tender, it is highly unlikely she would have appreciated the range of social practices bar work involves or been aware of the often tacit meanings and conventions that structure interactions with customers. She would certainly have had little insight into the more local and particular features that made up the social world of the pub in which the research took place. Without this understanding, Watson would clearly have risked imposing her own values and assumptions on to bar work. Thus, for interpretivist sociologists, there is little to be gained from the attempt to stand 'outside' one's object of study, in the manner of the natural scientist. What is needed is for the sociologist to get *involved* with that object in order to understand it properly.

SUMMARY OF SECTION 7

1   Diane Watson's ethnographic research illustrates the ways in which, for interpretivists, the objects of sociological enquiry are best understood as the outcome of meaningful human activity – that is, as being made and remade in the small-scale social interactions that take place in local social sites.

2   Its use of a participant observation method also illustrates the emphasis placed by interpretivist sociologists on getting 'inside' the social worlds they study, in order to see them from the actor's point of view.

3   Many interpretivist sociologists are largely uninterested in generalizing from their findings or predicting future outcomes. Others seek to construct theoretical models that can be used to identify general patterns or trends.

8   What constitutes authoritative knowledge about the social world?

Having studied the chapter so far, you now have a detailed overview of the competing answers that positivism and interpretivism provide to the question, 'What constitutes authoritative knowledge about the social world?'. As stated in the chapter's introduction, while positivism and interpretivism do not exhaust the range of responses sociologists have developed to answer this question, they nevertheless open up some of the main areas of debate. By way of summarizing the chapter's arguments, this penultimate section aims to revisit them in relation to a number of themes that, if in submerged form, have structured our thinking throughout the preceding discussion. These are:

- *detachment* and *involvement;*
- *explanation* and *understanding;* and,
- *facts* and *values.*

8.1   Detachment and involvement

As you will know from earlier sections of this chapter, for positivists, authoritative knowledge is that generated by the *detached* observation and careful measurement of the objects of sociological enquiry. Advocates of this approach urge the use or adaptation of the experimental method to ensure that sociologists remain as detached as possible from their objects of enquiry, thus minimizing the risk that their values (that is, their preconceptions, personal prejudices and cultural assumptions) will interfere with their findings. It is on this basis that positivists assert the factual status and thus the authority of their research.

However, as you have seen, the concept of detachment runs into specific challenges when applied to the study of the social world. In particular, the subject–object problem and the often 'fuzzy' character of social phenomena mean that sociologists cannot easily stand 'outside' or detach themselves from the objects they study since (as illustrated by the discussion of pleasure in section 4.1), as members of society, they are part of those objects. Thus, sociologists can never find a truly neutral point of observation outside the social world.

Indeed, as was argued in section 6, there is a risk that, in seeking to address their objects of enquiry in a detached manner, sociologists will simply impose their own values and meanings on those objects. It is for this reason that interpretivist sociologists advocate close *involvement* with the local and particular aspects of the social world being studied (that is, immersing oneself in or getting 'inside' these). Indeed, for interpretivists, it is the understanding that arises from this close involvement that guarantees the authority of the knowledge they produce.

8.2   Explanation and understanding

As the previous paragraph begins to suggest, the interpretivist emphasis on understanding and involvement – on 'beginning from the actor's point of view' – has proved highly productive in questioning positivist assumptions about the 'given' or objective nature of social phenomena (for example, that fear of crime is an objective entity with a single shared meaning). However, it is possible to argue that, despite its advantages, this emphasis – if pushed too far – risks evacuating important sociological terrain. We can begin to get a sense of what is at stake here from the following description of the centrality of quantitative methods to the history of feminist struggles and wider social reform:

> Historical innovations in empiricist methodology such as the social survey were made primarily by people, including women, who sought policy-relevant knowledge as ammunition for social reform. Reformers such as Jane Addams, Harriet Martineau, Florence Nightingale and Beatrice Webb carried out social investigations which served the reformist cause by revealing the extent of poverty and inequality … Feminist social reformers advocated the need for statistics to demonstrate the conditions of women's lives. For example, … [i]n the campaign against women's exclusion from higher education, statistics were used to disprove the masculinist medical notion that education damaged women's health. … [More recently, the] extensive socio-demographic mapping of women's position that underscored second-wave feminism would not have been possible without large-scale quantitative surveys. … The underlying gendering of structural inequalities that occurs in most societies could not be discerned using qualitative methods on their own. Statistics derived from official records or from large-scale surveys continue to demonstrate the ways in which gender, class and ethnicity intersect as axes of discrimination.
>
> (Oakley, 2002, p.296)

As this quotation begins to suggest, a commitment to quantitative methods and to *explaining* the causes of social inequality is not something that should be given up lightly. Yet, this is precisely what at least stronger versions of interpretivism often seem to advocate. For strong interpretivist sociologists, the social world is radically diverse, transitory and inherently fragile (this is because they see it as being endlessly made and remade in local social interactions). Needless to say, while it would be possible to generate causal explanations in relation to such a world, they would be necessarily local and particular rather than generalizable to a wider population (since any explanation could only be relevant to the precise interaction to which it referred).

However, it is possible to argue that, in suggesting there is little that is regular or patterned about social phenomena, strong interpretivists are in error. In **social structure** particular, they risk ignoring the existence of a **social structure**. This refers to those wider or more fundamental elements of the social world (such as relations of class, gender and 'race' discussed in *Social Differences and Divisions*: **Braham and Janes, 2002**) that are relatively stable and persistent over time, and that can be said to shape and limit the 'open' character of the social worlds in which we live. While qualitative methods can be used to identify these 'structural' features of the social world (see section 7 above), as Ann Oakley argues, it seems likely that the wider dimensions and effects of the social structure can be most effectively grasped using quantitative approaches, in particular the social survey. In short, it is arguably these that best capture the dimensions of the social structure and *explain* its effects. While sociological explanations may never achieve the level of predictive accuracy that is possible in the natural sciences, they can still be highly effective in establishing relationships between variables (or, as in the example of higher education and women's health cited by Oakley, disproving spurious relationships), as well as in identifying general social patterns and trends.

It is, of course, positivism that has most strongly advocated searching for causal explanations of social phenomena and been most willing to address social structure as an objective entity. However, as noted on several previous occasions, we should remember that 'lighter' versions of interpretivism (like those associated with the work of Max Weber) also retain, if in a more diluted form, an attachment to quantitative methods and to explanation and prediction in sociological research. Oakley's critique is thus best understood as an attempt to highlight the limitations of strong interpretivist approaches rather than to defend positivism.

8.3   Facts and values

As noted above, the subject–object problem in sociological enquiry means that values cannot easily be excluded from sociological research. What, then, should sociologists do about their values? Should they, despite the subject–object problem, aspire to 'value freedom'? Should they, in contrast, adopt the more limited ambition of 'value neutrality'? Or should they fully embrace values by seeking to be politically and morally 'engaged'? These questions necessarily raise issues about the *purposes* of sociology, both as a practice and as a body of knowledge, as well as *ethical* questions about the role sociology should play in wider social, political and economic life. These issues will be addressed in more detail in subsequent chapters of this book. However, if only in a preliminary fashion, they can be usefully raised in relation to the concerns of the current chapter.

Value freedom – the belief in the separation of facts from values – is most closely associated with positivist sociology. However, because of the subject–object problem, it is, in strict terms, an impossibility in sociological research. Nevertheless, for positivist sociologists it continues to be a useful aspiration or goal. Positivists tend to argue that, if values cannot be excluded from sociological enquiry, their role can be at least *minimized* via the careful application of closed system analyses. The importance of this is that, from a positivist perspective, it allows sociologists to distinguish between factual knowledge and mere speculation, superstition or received wisdom. The purpose of sociology from this perspective is, then, the generation of 'facts' or objective 'truths' – a purpose that necessarily entails avoidance of speculation or political or moral opinion mongering.

As an interpretivist, Max Weber was necessarily sceptical about the possibility of holding facts and values separate (since, as we have seen, for Weber social 'facts' are not objective features of the natural world but the product of people attributing meaning to their activities). Nevertheless, he continued to hold to a notion of value freedom in the more limited sense that he felt sociology as a practice does not have as its purpose the justification or pursuit of moral and political goals (Weber, 1970/1918). The term 'value neutrality' captures this modified sense of value freedom, as Peter Hamilton explains:

> By value-neutrality, Weber seems to have intended … that sociologists should not openly proclaim their personal views on matters of social fact. They might well be able to point out the social consequences of poverty, such as poor health or high crime rates for instance, but they should not, as sociologists, then use those social facts to advocate whether that poverty should be eradicated or that the poor should be more rigidly controlled by the police.
>
> (Hamilton, 2002b, p.15)

Note that this does not preclude sociologists from holding moral or political views. It merely suggests that the pursuit of these is not part of sociology's function – they belong to other spheres of activity.

In contrast to both the concepts of value freedom and value neutrality, the notion of political and moral engagement suggests that sociologists can and should be involved in active attempts to change the world around them. Derived, in part, from a 'critical', often Marxist, sociological tradition (such as that **Frankfurt School** associated with the **Frankfurt School**) and influenced by the radical political **feminism** movements (such as **feminism**, black power and gay liberation) emerging from the social upheavals of the 1960s and 1970s, advocates of moral and political engagement take a robust view of the role of values in sociological enquiry. One of the most famous statements of this position was made in an article, published in 1967, by the interpretivist sociologist Howard Becker (Becker, 1967). For Becker, it was not a question of, 'Should we take sides?' but, 'Whose side are we on?' (the title of his article). From this perspective, sociologists can never adopt a position of value neutrality since sociological knowledge inevitably informs the actions of powerful groups and institutions (such as governments and business corporations) and thereby shapes the social world. In response to this, advocates of political and moral engagement argue that sociologists should 'take sides', using sociological enquiry and knowledge as part of wider struggles to envisage and then realize the 'good society'.

In the light of this debate, it is clear that sociologists have taken up rather different positions in relation to the role of values in sociological enquiry, with positivists more likely to hold on to a notion of value freedom and, particularly since the 1960s, 'strong' interpretivists (like Becker) more likely to adopt a position of political and moral engagement. However, in drawing these conclusions, we need to inject a few notes of caution.

First, it is important to recognize that even strong interpretivists do not advocate an 'anything goes' approach to facts and values – one in which partisan positions override or replace careful and detailed research. After all, if you want to change something, it is important to have an accurate understanding of how it works. For example, despite having explicitly feminist aims, the ethnographer, Ann Whitehead (whom you came across in Reading 5.3 of *Understanding Everyday Life* – **Bennett and Watson, 2002a**) – and whose work was cited in section 4.3 of this chapter) will have paid scrupulous attention to the ways in which her pre-existing beliefs, assumptions and values may have shaped her perceptions of the The Wagonner and its regulars **(Whitehead, 1976)**. In short, while she would not expect to be able to exclude values from her research, she would expect to reflect on how these may have influenced her.

Second, while it is stronger interpretivist positions that have often been most closely associated with the concept of moral and political engagement, Ann Oakley's comments (quoted earlier in section 8.2) on the significance of the social survey in bringing about social reform, alert us to the fact that sociologists working with quantitative methods need not, of necessity, adopt a strong position on value freedom. Indeed, although often using quantitative methods, 'light' interpretivists will have a strong grasp of the ways in which the knowledge generated by these continues to be shaped by wider values and social meanings and the need to be alert to the consequences of this (see Chapter 3 of this volume for the way in which, for instance, quantitative data can be understood as a social product). Conversely, Weber's concept of value neutrality underlines the fact that not all sociologists working in the interpretivist tradition will necessarily adopt a position of moral or political engagement.

SUMMARY OF SECTION 8

1   Positivist sociology bases its claim to generate authoritative knowledge on the *detached* observation and measurement of the relationship between variables in a closed system. Interpretivist sociologists suggest that the subject–object problem renders the notion of detached observation problematic. They argue that, because social phenomena are the outcome of meaningful human activity, it is necessary for the researcher to be *involved* with his or her object of study in order to *understand* it.

2   Interpretivists argue that detachment risks imposing the researcher's own values and assumptions on to the object of enquiry. This suggests that *understanding* is central to the generation of authoritative sociological knowledge. However, a focus on understanding alone – particularly in the absence of attempts to build *explanations* and make predictions about future outcomes – risks failing to address the effects of social structure.

3   Sociologists have adopted competing approaches to the question of what they should do with their *values*. These include the advocacy of value freedom, value neutrality and moral and political engagement.

9   Conclusion

In the course of this chapter, you have explored two competing positions – positivism and interpretivism – each providing rival accounts of what constitutes authoritative knowledge about the social world. This has necessarily involved a detailed exploration of the precise *nature* of social phenomena (are they objective entities equivalent to those studied in the natural sciences?) and the *underlying principles* that inform competing ways of studying them (should sociologists be detached from or involved with their objects of enquiry; should they aim to explain or understand the social world; should they seek to minimize the role of values in their work or adopt a position of moral and political engagement?).

As suggested in the Introduction to this book, debates about the nature of social phenomena refer to questions of ontology (what we believe to exist), while debates about the principles that should guide our study of social phenomena refer to questions of epistemology (how we come to know about what we believe to exist). In the next two chapters of this book, you will be moving on from an exploration of such underlying principles to investigate the precise methods by which sociologists study the social world. Needless to say, we have already touched on methods in the course of this chapter (as well as elsewhere in DD201). However, Chapters 2 and 3 provide you with a more detailed introduction to them.

Before you move on to study Chapters 2 and 3, it is probably worth noting one final thing. You will remember that, in the previous section, it was suggested that the stance sociologists take on the role of values in their research raises, in turn, important ethical questions. For example, the decision as to whether sociologists should, in Becker's terms, 'take sides', particularly in struggles between the powerful and the subordinated, is a profoundly ethical one. Is it ethical to risk corrupting scientific neutrality? Or is it more ethical to seek to protect the weak from the strong? As you will discover, Chapters 2 and 3 (as well as the audio-visual materials that accompany the module) raise a number of more detailed questions about the role of ethics in research, while Chapter 4 returns to broader ethical questions about the purposes of sociology.

References

Becker, H. (1967) 'Whose side are we on?', *Social Problems*, vol.13, no.3, pp.239–47.

Bennett, T. and Watson, D. (eds) (2002a) *Understanding Everyday Life*, Oxford, Blackwell/The Open University.

Bennett, T. and Watson, D. (2002b) 'Understanding everyday life: Introduction' in Bennett, T. and Watson, D. (eds) *op. cit*.

Braham, P. and Janes, L. (eds) (2002) *Social Differences and Divisions*, Oxford, Blackwell/The Open University.

Bryman, A. (1988) *Quantity and Quality in Social Research*, London, Unwin Hyman.

Campbell, D.T. and Ross, H.L. (1968) 'The Connecticut crackdown on speeding: time-series data in quasi-experimental analysis', *Law and Society Review*, vol.3, pp.33–53.

Comte, A. (1971) 'The positive philosophy' in Thompson, K. and Turnstall, J. (eds) *Sociological Perspectives*, Harmondsworth, Penguin/The Open University. (First published in 1838.)

Denzin, N.K. and Lincoln, Y. (1994) *Handbook of Qualitative Research*, London, Sage.

Durkheim, E. (1951/1897) *Suicide: A Study in Sociology* (trans. J.A. Spaulding, ed. and with introduction by G. Simpson), Glencoe, IL, Free Press. (First published in 1897.)

Hamilton, P. (2002a) 'The street and everyday life' in Bennett, T. and Watson, D. (eds) *op. cit*.

Hamilton, P. (2002b) 'Mapping the field' in Hamilton, P. and Thompson, K. (eds) *The Uses of Sociology*, Oxford, Blackwell/The Open University.

Hamilton, P. and Thompson, K. (2002) 'The uses of sociology: Introduction' in Hamilton, P. and Thompson, K. (eds) *ibid.*

Hareven, T. (1993) 'The home and the family in historical perspective' in Bennett, T. and Watson, D. (eds) *op. cit.*

Hollway, W. and Jefferson, T. (2000) *Doing Qualitative Research Differently*, London, Sage.

Mead, G.H. (1934) *Mind, Self and Society*, Chicago, IL, Chicago University Press.

Oakley, A. (2002) 'Gender, methodology and people's ways of knowing' in Hamilton, P. and Thompson, K. (eds) *op. cit.*

Outhwaite, W. (2000) 'The philosophy of social science' in Turner, B.S. (ed.) *The Blackwell Companion to Social Theory*, Oxford, Blackwell.

Parr, J. (2002) DD201 *Sociology and Society*, 'Methods Booklet 4', Milton Keynes, The Open University.

Raistrick, D., Bradshaw, J., Tober, G., Winer, J., Allison, J. and Healey, C. (1994) 'Development of Leeds Dependency Questionnaire (LDQ): a questionnaire to measure alcohol and opiate dependence in the context of treatment and evaluation package', *Addiction*, vol.89, pp.563–72.

Redman, P. (2002) 'Love is in the air: romance and the everyday' in Bennett, T. and Watson, D. (eds) *op. cit.*

Rex, J. and Moore, R. (1967) *Race, Community and Conflict*, Oxford, Oxford University Press.

Sapsford, R. (1996) 'Reading quantitative research' in Sapsford, R. (ed.) *Researching Crime and Criminal Justice*, Milton Keynes, The Open University.

Savage, M. (2002) 'Social exclusion and class analysis' in Braham, P. and Janes, L. (eds) *op. cit.*

Shaw, C. (1930) *The Jack-Roller: A Delinquent Boy's Own Story*, Chicago, IL, University of Chicago Press.

Smith, M.J. (1998) *Social Science in Question*, London, Sage/The Open University.

Thomas, W.I. and Znaniecki, F. (1918/19/20) *The Polish Peasant in Europe and America*, Chicago, IL, University of Chicago Press, 1918, 1919; Boston, MA, Badger Press, 1920.

Watson, D. (2001) 'Learning the ropes in a dipsomaniac's paradise' in Bennett, T. and Watson, D. (eds) *op. cit.*

Watson, D. (2002) '"Home from home": the pub and everyday life' in Bennett, T. and Watson, D. (eds) *op. cit.*

Weber, M. (1968) *Economy and Society: An Outline of Interpretive Sociology* (ed. G. Roth and C. Wittich), New York, Bedminster. (First published in 1922.)

Weber, M. (1970) 'Science as a vocation' in Weber, M. *From Max Weber: Essays in Sociology* (trans. and ed. H.H. Gerth and C. Wright Mills), London, Routledge. (First published in 1918.)

Whitehead, A. (1976) 'Sexual antagonism in Herefordshire' in Bennett, T. and Watson, D. (eds) *op. cit.*

Yates, S. (2004) *Doing Social Science Research*, London, Sage/The Open University.

Reading

1.1 Diane Watson, 'Learning the ropes in a dipsomaniac's paradise' (2001)

I arrive at the pub with a sense of trepidation. I am thinking of what I have read in those occupational sociology studies about the struggle people have in 'learning the ropes' when starting a new kind of work. But soon I am taking up my position for the first time behind the bar. And Alex, the pub manager, watches as I pull my first pint. I do this remarkably easily and apparently very well. I later learn that this is the best first pint that Alex has ever seen pulled! The skill, I realize, lies in going slowly and not being rushed by anyone. Lager is a different technique but again, I find it is not too difficult. The point with the beer is to try to spill as little as possible whilst giving the customer a full pint with a good head. Some customers will ask for a flat pint and then the tap is taken off. This is also the case with shandy.

So, things aren't going too badly. But Alex then begins a run down of all the other drinks in the cabinets and in the optics. I need to know the prices of all these. I feel overwhelmed. I'll never remember all this information. The price of ales and lagers are on the pumps but a lot of them are not readable. Alex cleans them up and writes them in for me. But there are no prices on the bottles in the fridges and there seems to be quite a variation. How am I going to cope with all of this? The tills are manual and therefore a lot of adding up has to be done in the head. Alex points out that it is important that the bar worker makes customers confident about their ability to charge the correct price and to add up correctly. It is unlikely they will notice if I get it wrong, apparently. But they'll soon want to avoid me if I don't appear to know what I am doing.

However busy the bar gets I shouldn't allow the customers to hurry me, I'm told. That is when I'll begin to make mistakes. Alex shows me how to prioritize tasks in a busy bar. This is outlined in the pub company's new staff induction document. As part of my research I have managed to get hold of a copy if this. But Alex tells me he doesn't really use it. I should deal with the customers first, he says. I should then collect glasses and put them through the glass-washer, stacking the clean ones when I can. Cleaning the tables and the ashtrays comes last. I should always try to indicate that I have seen the next customer who is waiting to be served so that they know that I will be coming to them next.

The 11 am opening time is fast approaching but before the hands on the clock behind the bar reach 11, a couple come in and ask for coffee. Someone else, to my relief, serves them. But the hour strikes and I am on my own to face my first customer. I feel pretty anxious, telling myself that all sorts of other people do this so there is no reason why I shouldn't. But this doesn't help me very much. Customers begin to come in. Joe, one of the bar staff, is very reassuring and offers to give me help, should I need it. He helps me most, in fact, by taking the first couple of customers. But this is only a temporary respite.

Facing my first customer makes me feel awful. It is very embarrassing. But I make myself go forward and nervously greet the next one to approach the bar. I imagine that they somehow know how stupid I feel. But of course they cannot. And, indeed, my first pint goes well. In fact I am soon finding the pulling of pints physically very satisfying. And, to my relief, I am coping well with adding up the rounds. The problems come when people begin to order all the 'silly drinks' from the cabinets and I find I can't keep a track on the total as I fumble around for these odd concoctions. I keep a notepad for the till for emergencies but I am amazed how people are prepared to hand over their money even when I haven't yet come up with a total. Before long, though, I start to get confused and nearly overcharge a couple of women. They soon put me straight on the total, though. This means that I end up with an 'over-ring' and I have to start again. In my confusion I even try to hand the money back to them. They look at me blankly. I apologize and explain that I am new today. They are fine.

I carry on pulling pints and find myself thinking how easy it would be if it were all like this. However, I then notice that the Pedigree is very flat and I can't get a satisfactory head on it. I don't like giving it to the customers like this so I experiment with doing a top up. This works but I feel guilty about the beer I am wasting. Then I get totally confused when a customer offers me a drink. Alex hasn't briefed me on this. I try to decline the offer but the customer insists. I am rescued by Alex who tells me about the staff drinks book, pointing out that I can put the drink 'by' for later or another day and don't have to drink at work. I regain my composure and continue to pull the pints, relieved that it is simple pints that most people want.

I pour a pineapple juice for a young woman who points out that is not mixed. I feel totally stupid, realizing that the jugs have enclosed tops and that I should have shaken the jug before serving. Why do I seem to lose my common sense in this situation? My worst moment comes, however, when an obviously romantically involved couple arrives. The man asks for a Martini and lemonade but I can't even find the Martini, never mind serve it. When I do find the drink I notice that there is no price on it. And the optic won't work for me either. It is a type of optic I haven't seen before and clearly the training doesn't extend to experimenting with spirits. I am lost but explain that I am under training and that I need to wait for the expert to come and show me. Alex helps out but I am now 'set up' with this customer, exactly as Alex warned might happen. I am now a novice, publicly and visibly, and for this 'pushy' customer nothing is going to be right. He soon decides that his glass is the wrong size. He also announces that the draught cider I poured earlier has gone flat. Alex goes to check the barrel but there is nothing wrong with it. And, as I thought, draught cider is pretty flat anyway. However, this illustrates to me that confidence in the bar staff is crucial to successful service. I am learning the ropes.

An interesting thing that I begin to notice is just how nervous and awkward so many customers are. Out of the corner of my eye I catch sight of a strange and unusual looking man. He looks to be in his sixties and is he wearing a grey suit. His skin is very brown and he has a long grey ponytail. He drinks a pint or two before ambling over to look at the range of our beers. I ask if I can help and he ponders on what he might want. 'I just need to browse for a while', he explains, 'it's a dipsomaniac's dream in here.' This makes my day.

On my second day I arrive at 10 am and use what I learned on the previous occasion to get the bar ready for serving. I'm feeling pretty confident now about finding my way around the bars and knowing what needs to be done. I'm still afraid of the coffee machine, however, and dread the arrival of the first customers. I spend some time writing up the prices of drinks in my notebook so that I can try to learn them before the customers start coming. I leave this by the till as an aide-mémoire. I wonder whether it will work. The sun is out and it is Friday. This means it is likely to get busy. Today I am working with Suzanne who is doing a languages degree and Dan in the kitchen is a maths graduate who is thinking of doing a PhD. They are all interested in my academic background and Nigel is very keen to be interviewed by me.

It is quiet until about 12.30. Someone then comes in and asks me if she has enough money for an orange and soda. Unfortunately she hasn't and she is very 'put out' by me. I am tempted to give it to her anyway but realize that I can't. I give her a glass of iced water instead. Only afterwards do I realize that she works at the theatre to which the pub is attached and that, with discount, she could have had the drink. Nigel says she is always grumpy anyway so not to worry. She comes back later for another drink of water and I apologize for not knowing who she was. She is very friendly and introduces herself to me and asks my name. All of a sudden, at that point however, customers begin to come in thick and fast. Some are regulars and talk to each other as they order the rounds. This makes it hard to remember what they want and even harder to add up the bill. Others come in large crowds and have huge orders. The theatre press officer comes in with a client. She knows that I am new and introduces herself to me. She has an account but I don't know anything about how it works. I just serve her and make a note of her bill to sort it out with Nigel afterwards.

I'm not yet sinking in this flood of customers but I do have a problem remembering all the prices. I feel really bad if I have to interrupt a colleague to ask a price, especially if they have been adding up a large round themselves and find themselves losing it because of me. Nevertheless I have learnt a lot from yesterday and don't make the same mistakes I made then. Rushing back and forth between the bars I worry about someone slipping on the kitchen floor. There is spilt mayonnaise and I skid in it. No one seems to have time or be concerned, so I decide to stop to mop it up with napkins and cover the dangerous spot on the floor. Coincidentally, I pick up on a conversation between the staff in the other bar about the floor in the main bar.

> 'This slippery floor is dangerous for our customers.'
>
> 'I know. We have a responsibility to protect our customers from injury and someone will slip on this.'
>
> 'Well, I have told Alex and he is in charge so the buck stops with him.'
>
> 'Yes, but we are all responsible if something happens, aren't we?'

It is now extremely busy and the pace of orders in the kitchen is frantic. There is no soup. It hasn't defrosted. This doesn't go down well with the serving staff. We have to remember to delete items from the board as they are sold out and we are not popular if we forget to let people know when the last cob of a particular filling has been sold. I am not making a very good job of my order dockets, largely because I don't think I have worked out what is done with these after the order has been placed. I give out ticket numbers but Suzanne has failed to give one to all the people she has served. Outside is a sea of faces and you just can't remember who ordered what, however hard you try. A woman complains that she has been waiting ages for her baguette and she hasn't got a ticket number. She wasn't given one. We work out that her order is in the queue and Mary says that her baguette is next. About half an hour later the same women apprehends me as I am delivering an order, reminding me that her order is next. I know this order I am carrying is designated for someone else but can't pass her over again. I feel awful for her so I give her one of the baguettes thinking I'll deal with the problem in a moment. This then causes consternation in the kitchen but miraculously we find a matching order and everyone is then happy. This confusion wasn't my fault but, being new, I am sure people thought it was. Anyway, I think that some of the subsequent confusions that arise are down to me. I make a mental note always to give out a ticket number and always to put the order on the spike so they know in the kitchen what they have sold. I know I have lost

some tickets and that means that they won't have a record in the kitchen of what has been sold. I remember a conversation with Nigel about the importance of good stock control and I will lose a lot of sleep that night thinking about whether I have messed anything up.

It is clear that training really ought to go right back to essentials. In my case things have been assumed which shouldn't have been. But I will know next time how to handle it. It has been so busy that I have not been able to collect glasses and am really worried that we will run out. We don't. As the pace slackens off I start to collect glasses and clean things up. Amazingly, I am all cleared up before 3 pm. I have survived the rush of a busy Friday lunchtime.

It seems that I have done quite well. It is readily agreed that I should experience a busy Friday night soon. Nigel tells Tony, when Tony arrives to collect me, that I have been a great help. He assures Tony that he is not just being polite. I really have done well. I am so pleased with myself. And later that week Magnus, who organised my participant observation access, says, 'You will be gratified to know that Alex Porter is very pleased with his new member of staff. You have fitted in really well. It seems that you worked really hard and that the job is yours any time you want it.' Phew!

Source: **Watson, 2001, pp.225–8**

2

Qualitative sociological research

Elizabeth B. Silva and Janet Parr

Contents

1   Introduction

The introduction to this book suggested that an understanding of social research methods is important, not because as part of this module you will be asked to undertake research of your own, but because any critical appreciation and evaluation of sociological texts requires knowledge of how those texts were produced.

methodology

As the introduction also argued, the study of how sociologists, and others, go about their work – how they conduct investigations, assess evidence and decide what constitutes authoritative knowledge – is referred to as **methodology**. Methodology involves a wide range of issues, many of which were outlined in Chapter 1. These include, among many others, debates about the scientific status of social scientific knowledge; whether laws exist in the social sciences which can predict, as well as explain, whether research can, or should, be free of values, morals and political involvement; and the relationships that exist between cause and effect in social situations and contexts. In contrast, the study of *what we are doing*, or should be doing, when we investigate something involves consideration of research *methods*. It is, then, these methods upon which we will be focusing in this and the following chapter, with qualitative approaches addressed in this chapter and quantitative approaches in Chapter 3.

As you will discover, we take the position that, despite the 'war of paradigms' between positivism and interpretivism, there is much in common between qualitative and quantitative approaches since they are both forms of knowledge shaped by the social contexts in which they are produced. Indeed, it is possible to argue that the key to good sociology is not whether it is based on quantitative or on qualitative methods. This dualism is not helpful. As Oakley (2002, p.296) states, qualitative research is not more authentic than quantitative, nor is it more ethical. The critical issue is whether research is undertaken according to open and systematic criteria that other people can inspect. The crucial questions for both doing and inspecting social research are: What is known? What values, perceptions and beliefs are brought into what is known? How are these known? Central to these questions is the claim that what is known and the act of knowing are intrinsically linked. In consequence, you perhaps won't be surprised to discover that, even if sociological quantitative research is nowadays the least used method, there is currently considerable 'methodological pluralism', as a study of sociological research methods used in sociology journals in the UK discovered in 2004 (Payne *et al.*, 2004).

Qualitative research comprises a large and heterogeneous body of knowledge. It has grown out of a wide range of traditions, some of which you have come across elsewhere in DD201 – see, for instance, the discussion in section 5 of Chapter 7 in *Understanding Everyday Life* (**Hemmings *et al.*, 2002**). As with other research methods, qualitative research refers to data generation techniques and procedures; to the selection of data sources and

Figure 2.1 *Ann Oakley*

'sampling' (discussed further below); and to the analysis and presentation of data. In this chapter we concentrate on three different aspects of qualitative research: interviewing (in section 2), ethnography (in section 3) and the use of documentary and visual material (in section 4). We then move on to consider issues of ethics in research (in section 5) and bring the chapter to a close by examining issues of validity and generalizability (in section 6).

AIMS

The aims of this chapter are:

1 To look at ways in which sociology is carried out by use of qualitative research methods.

2 To examine three aspects of qualitative research:

  (a) interviews (focusing in particular on semi-structured interviews)

  (b) ethnography (focusing in particular on participant observation)

  (c) documentary and visual material.

3 To consider issues of ethics in research and problems of validity and generalizability.

---

2   Qualitative interviewing

Qualitative interviewing refers to a range of techniques that involve asking people questions with the aim of understanding their local social worlds from the 'inside' or 'starting from their own point of view' (see Chapter 1, section 6). Qualitative interviews can sometimes be very informal – for instance, an impromptu chat which nevertheless illuminates something the researcher had previously misunderstood. However, the term more often refers to a relatively formal process in which the researcher meets with one or more participants face-to-face and encourages them to talk at length and 'from their own point of view' – that is, drawing on the meanings, values, forms of cultural classification and so forth that are current in their social world.

When employing qualitative interviewing techniques, both the knowledge and the evidence generated are contextual, situational and, as we have just implied, interactional. This means that, because each interview is carried out in a way that is sensitive to each particular situation, qualitative interview techniques in turn must be flexible. A clear assumption of qualitative interviews is that the interview itself is not separate from the social interaction in which it is produced. It is a particular kind of conversation, with a specific aim in mind; Burgess (1984, p.2) refers to such interviews as 'conversations with a purpose'. But, what kind of conversation is an interview? Interviewing is concerned with asking specific questions related to a particular research topic and eliciting meaningful answers to those questions. Interviews may be carried out for different purposes and follow different styles. The in-depth and semi-structured styles of interviewing, usually associated with qualitative research, are particular techniques for generating data. The semi-structured interview is the most common technique used in qualitative research.

The term 'semi-structured' refers to a range of interview situations, from a combination of structured and **open-ended questions**, to a situation in which the interview is relatively unstructured: an interviewer may start a conversation in a particular direction, but will then allow the conversation to develop according to cues taken from what is said by the respondent. It is rare, if not impossible, for an interview to be totally unstructured, however. Both researchers and the people they are talking with – the participants or interviewees – will have some idea of what the interview is going to be about, so the setting and the topic of conversation at least are loosely predefined. With semi-structured interviewing, researchers enter the interview situation with an idea of the topics to be covered, but are free to modify the order and the approach, based on their perception of what is most appropriate in any given situation, and according to the responses made. Interviewers can alter the way in which questions are worded, can change the order, leave out particular questions if they do not seem appropriate, and can allow the conversation to develop within areas raised by the respondent. The interviewee is allowed to take the discussion down avenues which the interviewer may not have considered. This can prove hugely advantageous, because it may reveal data that had not been anticipated.

2.1   The semi-structured interview technique

As mentioned above, sometimes, a very open interview structure is used and researchers will simply ask one or two stimulating questions or make one or two comments and take the discussion forward from what develops. This was the approach taken by **Peter Redman (2002)** in the research outlined in Chapter 2 of *Understanding Everyday Life* **(Bennett and Watson, 2002a)** and we shall look at this in more detail now. Redman writes:

> … we will be exploring material from qualitative interviews that I conducted in the early 1990s with a group of ten 16- to 18-year-old boys. Qualitative interviewing is generally small in scale and attempts to 'get inside' the social worlds of interviewees in order to gain an insight into the meanings they give to them. Thus, the interview material discussed here does not claim to be representative of a wider population (you may or may not recognize your own experience in it). What it aims to show is how the respondents lived, talked and felt about their heterosexual relationships in the very specific context of their sixth-form college.
>
> …
>
> The interview material was collected as part of a wider ethnographic research project (conducted with Debbie Epstein and Gurjit Minhas and funded by East Birmingham Health Authority) that explored the sexual cultures of 11- to 14-year-old young people in secondary schools (see Epstein and Johnson, 1998). My primary aim in interviewing the older group of boys was to get them to reflect on their experiences at a younger age. However, in the course of the interviews, the boys tended to talk about current or more recent relationships as well as their experiences in the earlier years of secondary school, and I rapidly became interested in hearing about these.
>
> …
>
> The interviews lasted between forty-five and one hundred and twenty minutes and were taped and transcribed. All but one of the interviews was conducted in a private room at the college during the boys' free time. Eight of the boys chose to be interviewed individually, two chose to be interviewed in a pair.

Five follow-up interviews were conducted with four of the boys. The purpose of the research was explained to the boys and they volunteered to be interviewed in the light of this. Their confidentiality was assured and, in conducting the interviews, I took care to distinguish myself from adults teaching in the college by dressing informally.

(Redman, 2002, pp.59–60)

As Redman explains in the PhD thesis upon which Chapter 2 of *Understanding Everyday Life* was based, before interviewing the boys, he spent two days in the college in order to familiarize himself with the surroundings and the student culture. A total of fourteen interviews were then carried out over two phases – a first phase of nine interviews (one with two boys) and a second of five. The interviews were tape recorded and transcribed, and they followed a 'conventional "open" qualitative format' (Redman, 1999, p.122).

ACTIVITY 1

Make a note of what you think are the important points about qualitative interviewing.

Although so far we have focused on Redman's research, and some of the points raised have been specific to his work, some general issues have also emerged and we want to discuss these in relation to wider research practices. They include:

- Interviewing was small-scale and face-to-face.
- A conventional 'open' qualitative format was adopted.
- Privacy and confidentiality were assured.
- The sample size was small, so cannot be representative of a wider population.
- The boys volunteered to be interviewed.
- The interviewer dressed informally.
- Interviewing was largely about discovering meanings in context.

Interviewing was small-scale and face-to-face with an 'open' format. Redman's intention was to gain depth of information about the boys' attitudes towards intimate relationships, so his aim was to talk with them on a one-to-one basis in a relatively unstructured way. 'Relatively unstructured' or 'open' means that no formal schedule, or list, of questions is used, although researchers do generally have a list of topics that they want to cover. For instance, Redman's interviews followed a loose agenda which included topics such as: current or recent girlfriend/boyfriend relationships; relationships occurring in earlier years of schooling; the cultures of the secondary schools that participants had previously attended; and the extent and nature of homophobia both in the college and in secondary schools previously attended.

Within such a loose framework, interviewees are usually free to speak as they wish and the interview tends to follow a much more natural 'conversational' format, which will vary with each person involved. A problem the researcher may face is keeping the interviewee to the topic that the researcher wants to discuss, although this will generally be disclosed before the interview begins. In this quite intimate setting, it is important that researchers establish a comfortable working relationship with the people they are interviewing, in order to facilitate an easy exchange and truthful information. It is interesting that two of the boys chose to be interviewed together. Do you think this would have made any difference to what they said in the interview? We cannot assess this from the material available, but we can expect that the presence of another person would change the dynamics of the interview situation and would undoubtedly have had an effect on accounts.

Essential to a comfortable working relationship is the issue of confidentiality – participants need to know that what is said is going to be treated with respect, that their names will not be divulged to anyone else and that the material gathered will not be used for any purpose other than that of the research. In Redman's research both *privacy and confidentiality were assured*. Privacy and confidentiality are important to the generation of honest and reliable data. If participants are fairly certain that privacy will be guarded, then they are more likely to be relaxed and open about their views and feelings in the interview. Confidentiality is generally protected by the use of pseudonyms and by the disguising of other detail such as geographical location and the name of any establishment connected with the interviewee.

The sample size was small, so cannot be representative of a wider population. Sampling is an important part of all social research. We discuss this in more detail in Chapter 3, but, briefly, a sample is a small part of a larger group or population. Although sampling is commonly associated with statistical modes of quantitative research, strategic sampling, based on theoretical principles and on the purposes of the investigation, is most relevant to qualitative studies. (Theoretical principles are the main points in the theory guiding the research.) Theoretical sampling strategies can respond to different rationales, where selection of a particular 'adequate sample' is made on the basis of the capacity of selected respondents (or participants) to take forward the analysis in a specific way, helping either to confirm or refute the theoretical ideas linked to the research. In the case of Redman's research the sample size was very small and located in a particular school in a specific part of the UK. Because the sample was not representative – that is, it did not cover all groups of students in the school, or include a range of schools and areas which were representative of the country (or an area as a whole), it is not possible to say with any validity that the findings can be related to a wider population. However, it was not the intention of the project to produce 'generalizable' claims of this kind, but to gain an insight into the behaviour of a particular group of boys. (We look more closely at generalizability in section 6 of this chapter, and at both representativeness and generalizability in section 3.3 of Chapter 3.) The benefit of this type of qualitative data is in the richness of the personal material, which would be difficult to gain with any other research method.

The boys volunteered to be interviewed. Without people being willing to be part of social investigation, it would be impossible to conduct any research effectively. What attracts research participants may vary widely. For instance, in a study conducted by one of the authors of this chapter and based on 25 **focus groups** selected to represent a particular cross-section of the British population, financial incentives were attractive to the unemployed, while researchers were advised against offering these to older people, who were instead offered refreshments and biscuits. Wine was regarded as proper to offer to professionals, and the person assembling together the group of gay men thought money should not be offered but advised on wine, beer and nibbles (Silva, 2004).

focus groups

However, in addition to tangible inducements and attractions, participants in research projects may also have elusive motivations of different kinds. For example, there is the danger that those who volunteer will have a particular interest in the project and a particular story to tell. (Those who *don't* volunteer could well have presented a different story.) The implication of this is that it is not possible to relate the results to a wider population with any certainty. As this suggests, selection is always a problem in research, whether this is selection by the interviewer, or self-selection by the person being interviewed. Different strategies to attract participation bring about different problems for the research and the point is to be aware of these and, as far as possible, monitor their impact on the data generated.

The interviewer dressed informally. Redman found it important to distinguish himself from the teachers in the college by dressing informally. Similarly, when one of the authors of this chapter was researching for her PhD, she dressed formally when interviewing top managers in the headquarters of Ford of Europe, and informally when interviewing shop-floor workers in Dagenham (Silva, 1988). In a college, as in other similar situations, a power imbalance exists between staff and students; Redman's dressing informally was therefore an attempt to *distance* himself from the school staff and create an interview environment in which the boys would feel more confident to talk openly about their feelings. Researchers attempt to create as natural or neutral a setting as possible in which to talk with people, so that the outcome of the interview is shaped as little as possible by either the researcher or the surroundings. However neutral the setting, though, a power imbalance will exist in the interview situation and this will inevitably influence what is said. As Redman argued: 'Interviewees' responses are never simply passive reflections of something that exists outside the interview room, but are also produced in the context of the interview itself, and are shaped by the interviewee's perception of his or her addressee' (Redman, 1999, p.151).

In view of these issues, does the material gathered in the interview reflect the external reality of the interviewee? Or is it simply a product of the interview process? Reactivity (that is, the way in which people react to one another in any social situation) happens in every interaction – we all react to and are influenced by one another in social interactions, and interviews are no exception. However, this does not mean that qualitative interviews are hopelessly 'biased' and unable to tell us anything about the world of the interviewee. In fact, although researchers need to reflect on how and why reactivity occurs in an interview, it can often provide them with much useful information.

Interviewing was largely about discovering meanings in context. Discovering meanings involves encouraging participants to talk about their attitudes and feelings on various topics. It is the job of the researcher to stimulate conversation in that direction. In his PhD thesis Redman (1999) tells of how he did this:

> … in the first round of nine interviews, basic demographic data about the interviewees were … obtained and the interview proper began with a 'generative', open question (Flick, 1998): 'Are you involved in a relationship at the moment? … Would you like to tell me about it?', or, 'Is there a relationship that you want to tell me about?'… this was designed to elicit a response from the boys in which they talked about boyfriend/girlfriend relationships in their

own time, and from within their own frameworks of meaning. … Major areas for discussion were typically opened up with an 'open' or 'non-directive' (Rogers, 1944) generative question (for example, 'Did anyone have a "girlfriend" when you were at primary school? … Could you tell me about this?'; 'What was your secondary school like?'; 'What is college like compared with your secondary school?'; 'Were there pupils who were routinely picked on at your secondary school. … Why was this?') and were followed up with further questions seeking clarification or a more in depth response to various points.

(Redman, 1999, p.132)

Even though the focus here is largely on the views of the respondents, the researcher is, to some extent, guiding and controlling the direction of the conversation, while also working to ensure that freedom of expression is facilitated. The very fact that the researcher seeks clarification or a more in-depth response to various points means that the interviews cannot be neutral. Care must be taken not to structure the interview so that the researcher gets what they want or expect, rather than data that emerge in a relatively unbiased and unpredicted way.

We can see from the points above that a qualitative interview is a flexible research tool which enables the probing and following up of interesting responses and topics that may lead to a number of further avenues of enquiry. The researcher has the difficult, and stimulating, task of listening, of thinking about what is being said, of picking up on interesting comments being made, and of remembering what has already been discussed. Recording the information can be a problem, and for this reason interviews are generally tape recorded and subsequently transcribed. It is important to gain permission from the interviewee for this, and also for taking notes if a tape recorder is not used.

Researchers must also watch for the body language of the person talking. As Robson (1993, p.229) argues: 'Non-verbal cues may give messages which help in understanding the verbal response, possibly changing, or even, in extreme cases, reversing its meaning.' Thus, an interview is not just 'a conversation with someone': it has a particular purpose and is structured in a particular way. It is important that researchers who use this method of data generation are aware not only of its strengths but also of some of the difficulties which may arise. Although we have focused largely on just one piece of work, some general points can be drawn out from what we have discussed.

ACTIVITY 2

Consider what the strengths and weaknesses of qualitative interviewing might be. Make some notes to clarify your thoughts.

Some of the *strengths* of qualitative interviewing are:

- The interview is flexible and adaptable to individual situations.
- Lines of enquiry can be modified and interesting points followed up.
- More in-depth data can be collected.
- Feelings and attitudes need to be noted by observing non-verbal cues as well by listening to verbal ones.
- A one-to-one personal relationship may elicit richer data than an anonymous situation, particularly where an element of trust has been established.

- If appropriate action is taken, the material generated will be driven by the person being interviewed, rather than by the interviewer.

- The interview provides potential for access to people's social worlds 'from the inside' – that is, from the perspective of the interviewee.

Some of the *weaknesses* of qualitative interviewing are:

- Good use of this flexible approach requires considerable interviewing skill and experience.

- The lack of a standardized approach may raise questions about the replicability (or reliability) of the material, since questions, or prompts, asked in a different way or in a different order, may elicit a different response. (Remember that, as discussed in Chapter 1, for positivists the ability to replicate findings is central to the production of authoritative knowledge.)

- Interviewing is time consuming and can therefore be costly. Not only is time needed for the interview, but also for reflecting on the interview, reviewing notes and/or transcribing the audio-taped recordings.

- Sample sizes tend to be small and local, making it difficult to generalize from the findings.

- Since qualitative interviews are also social interactions, there is a danger that the interviewer can affect the response by the way the question is framed, how a particular answer or comment is received, and even through their body language.

Although researchers need to be aware of the pitfalls associated with qualitative interviewing, the rich data generated by this method would be difficult to collect in any other way. We move now to consider the analysis of qualitative interview material.

2.2 Analysing qualitative interview material

Concern with analysis of interview material should not emerge only at the end stage of the research process. Analysing data is integral to the whole process and should be carried out before, during and after the interview material has been collected. You might ask, 'How can this be so'?

Before researchers embark on any primary data generation (that is, gaining knowledge on a first-hand basis), they will have read extensively about the topic and reflected on what the existing literature has (or has not) revealed. At this point analysis is already taking place: notes are made and ideas are jotted down. This is not a 'one-off' process, but is ongoing throughout the other phases of the research process, with a great deal of movement between existing documentary evidence and the emergent material. Reading, reflecting on and analysing interview data further informs the interviewing process. In the case of Redman's study, even before the interviews started considerable analysis of data had already been carried out as an ongoing part of the whole research. The interviews took place in two stages. Part of the initial round of nine interviews was aimed at collecting basic demographic and educational data, and was analysed numerically. This is often done in qualitative data generation in order both to provide the researcher with a better knowledge of the context of the investigation and to give the reader some means by which to assess the significance of the material in terms of validity and generalization. For instance, Redman noted that:

> All [the interviewees] self-identified as white English, and the majority came from what can be described as broadly middle-class or professional backgrounds. ... two of the ten interviewees identified themselves as having no experience of a sexual and/or romantic relationship, three as having had at least one girlfriend while at secondary school, while the five remaining participants identified themselves as being in a current relationship or as having been in the near past. ...

> All the boys were academically orientated in that they were studying for 'A' levels and expected to go on to higher education. Two of the boys ... were Oxbridge candidates.
>
> (Redman, 1999, p.123)

In the second phase of the interviews, the concern was solely with relationships, in particular with 'romance'. This concern emerged as a result of analysing the first round of interviews from which further questions emerged. At this stage, the topic could be refined and better focused:

> Since initial reading of the first round of transcripts suggested that the boys were talking about their relationships through the conventions of the romance genre, I also sought to identify whether the boys were 'reading' romance in an attempt to locate the relationship between the romance genre as a public cultural form and their apparent use of it to talk about (and live) their relationships.
>
> (Redman, 1999, p.134–5)

Looking back, we can see the interplay between data generation, reflection and analysis, right from the start of Redman's research. However, even this staged process is broken down into smaller stages.

During the actual data generation process, analysis goes on from the very first interview. Memory can be misleading and thoughts become coloured by the most recent interviews, so the skilled in-depth interviewer leaves time for reflection, as soon as possible after completion, on both the process and the content of the interview that has been completed. Thus, patterns begin to emerge and links between aspects of the material generated begin to be made.

It is impossible to carry all of the information in one's head, particularly with a large sample. It is necessary to sort the data so that clear connections and relationships within the data can be seen. The first stage in this process is working with the interview tapes or notes. Most, though not all, researchers choose to transcribe the tapes so that they have a 'hard copy' on which to work. Redman transcribed his tapes and coded the data:

> I recoded the interview transcripts by hand using a process of what Hammersley and Atkinson (1995: 185) refer to as 'coding the record', that is, identifying categories, themes, and examples on copies of the individual transcript pages, a process that helps retain the integrity and 'locatedness' of the interview interaction. At the end of every transcript, I produced a summary sheet, providing an overview of major themes and listing the coding categories and the page numbers on which these appeared. This enabled cross-referencing between transcripts.

> In this coding, I sought to identify any material related to romantic and/or sexual relationships with girls. From this process the following relevant categories emerged: 'types' or 'discourses' of sexual and emotional relationship described (for example, 'romance' or 'being in love', 'getting off' with someone at a party); cultural practices involved in romantic and/or sexual relationships (for example,

asking out, days out, 'going steady', writing letters and so on); narrative structures related to sexual and/or emotional relationships; and romance motifs or genre conventions related to sexual and/or emotional relationships.

(Redman, 1999, pp.142–3)

Good data management is essential in the short term – for ease of access and reliable use of the material in writing up the analysis and results of the investigation. In the long term, it is important that the claims and arguments developed on the basis of the research material be verified and, if necessary, the study repeated. As a critical reader of sociological studies, one also needs to bear in mind that what emerges from the analysis of the research material will be informed largely by the research questions and the way in which the data have been sorted and coded. Different questions and orientations are most likely to produce different analyses.

Good data management is also necessary if the researcher intends to use one of the computer software packages designed to assist with the coding and analyses of qualitative research material. Computer analysis of qualitative data has grown rapidly and newer software packages have emerged, aimed at facilitating the analysis of qualitative studies. Computer packages make the work of locating particular themes and issues much quicker, but tend to disrupt what, in the previous quotation, Redman refers to as 'the integrity and "locatedness"' of interview material. In other words, in extracting segments or individual words from the interview, computer packages can detract from the precise texture and meaning these acquire in relation to the interview as a whole. Many qualitative researchers also wish to retain the whole picture, and will often either work manually or, more often, with a combination of manual and computer analyses.

Let us now make links with the beginning of the research. The research starts with some general ideas, informed by experience and/or a literature review and analysis of the topic. This then generates more focused areas of interest and (loosely structured) research questions. These research questions inform the investigation of the topic of study: for example, by way of a semi-structured interview. The categorization and analysis of the interview material are related back to the original research ideas and questions. The researcher may then ask 'Are the original ideas borne out, or refuted, or has something completely different emerged?' Thus, the final analysis is structured by its relationship to the original research aims. Most research is undertaken for a specific purpose and the end-product is a report of one type or another, so once the data have been analysed, how should they be presented?

2.3 Presentation of analysed interview data

In qualitative data generation, a vast amount of rich and interesting narrative material is amassed. However, it is important to be selective in what is presented. If we look at Chapter 2 of *Understanding Everyday Life*, where Redman discusses his study, we can see that qualitative material is used in a variety of ways. To set the scene for the topic discussed in the chapter, two extracts are selected to illustrate commitment to heterosexual romance **(Redman, 2002, p.52)**. In the remainder of the chapter, there is a general discussion of particular aspects of the chosen topic, and often a reference to other research or writing which has been done in the field. This is then illustrated by the use of verbatim material from the research.

We have to trust to the professionalism of the author/researcher that the verbatim material used is an accurate representation of what has been said and that it illustrates the more general results of the research. This means investing considerable faith in the researcher, which is why an open and unambiguous report of the whole research procedure should be made available for scrutiny and criticism. This matters for the assessment of the validity of the claims made. However, what is selected as important in a research study will be determined by what the researcher considers to be important, or of value. As you saw in Chapter 1, this is, in turn, shaped by the underlying philosophical position the researcher adopts. What they consider to be of value will be determined by their perspective. The key issue of concern is that a researcher's ontological position is matched by their epistemological position. As you will remember from the Introduction to this book, **ontology** refers to that which we believe to exist in the social world we study, whereas **epistemology** refers to what we recognize as knowledge, or evidence of phenomena (the theory of knowledge).

ontology
epistemology

As we indicated above, it is also the case that qualitative data can be quantified and presented in numerical form. Often, qualitative research material is presented in a form indicating the views of 'most', 'the majority', 'more than', and so on; and trends are emphasized with expressions such as 'often' or 'frequently' (all quantitative expressions). Likewise, it is also worth remembering that quantitative analyses also use qualitative material. For instance, arguing against the sharp historical divide between quantitative and qualitative approaches, Oakley (2002) recounts that an accurate and detailed reading of social studies material of the late nineteenth century shows that 'counting' was often accompanied by the incorporation of the subjective viewpoint of those studied. We will, of course, be returning to some of the ways in which quantitative and qualitative methods overlap, in Chapter 3.

SUMMARY OF SECTION 2

1   Qualitative interviews are used to generate research material about people's knowledge, views, understanding and experiences.

2   Knowledge generated by employing qualitative approaches is contextual, situational and interactional.

3   Qualitative interviews are flexible and sensitive to each particular situation, and they are not separate from the interaction in which they are produced.

4   Semi-structured interviewing has been the most common technique used in qualitative research.

5   Although the research process is broken down into small parts, analysis is integral to the whole process, involving research questions, data generation techniques and the organization of research material. At the final analysis stage researchers make links with the original research aims.

6   The presentation of analysed interview data needs to be consistent with the original ideas and allow for the assessment of the claims made for validity.

3   Ethnography

Redman (2002) refers to the wider study, of which his qualitative interviews were a part, as an ethnographic study. **Ethnography** can broadly be defined as the study of the way of life, or of the culture, of a large community, a nation, or a small group of individuals. There is a great diversity of ethnographic research. Denzin and Lincoln (1994) write of 'five moments' in qualitative research which have affected the undertaking of ethnographic work. The first refers to programmes of research which, although qualitative, continued to uphold many positivist ideas about what constitutes authoritative knowledge. This 'moment' lasted from the 1900s to the Second World War and is generally associated with anthropology and the study of small-scale groups, and what have been defined as 'primitive' societies. For these studies researchers lived for lengthy periods with the groups they were studying, learning their language and culture and interpreting behaviour, customs and traditions from the perspective of the groups. The second moment is associated with the work of the Chicago School during the 1930s, which adopted anthropological methods to study their own city (see **Hamilton (2002)** and **Pile (2002)**; the history of ethnography is also sketched in **Bennett and Watson (2002b)** and **Hemmings *et al.* (2002)**). Employing ethnographic methods of data generation, the Chicago School produced rich qualitative data on the lives of a range of social groups, though the emphasis tended to be on poor people and those defined as 'deviant'. This type of research fell out of popularity in sociology during the 1950s, but emerged again in the 1960s with the work of **Howard Becker** and **Erving Goffman** in the USA, and in the UK with the work of **Stuart Hall** and his co-authors at the Centre for Contemporary Cultural Studies in Birmingham. This third 'moment' spans the late 1960s to the mid 1980s. These studies encompass a multiplicity of theoretical orientations described by Denzin and Lincoln (1994) in terms of 'blurred genres'.

ethnography

Becker, Howard
Goffman, Erving
Hall, Stuart

Figure 2.2   *Immigrants arriving in the USA: immigrant life was one of the areas studied by Chicago School researchers pioneering the use of ethnographic and qualitative methods*

Diverse ways of collecting data combined qualitative interviewing with observational, visual and documentary methods and personal experience. Computers were also entering the scene at this time. The fourth moment is characterized mainly by the erosion of the previous canons of truth creation and method, including the idea that ethnographies can simply reflect the truth of a culture. The moral and intellectual authority of ethnographers was challenged. In the fifth, and current, moment, diversity continues. In line with the broad interpretivist position identified in Chapter 1, ethnography is now fragmented, with some researchers adopting 'strong' interpretivist positions, some building on positivist precepts, and some adopting a pragmatic eclectic approach (Lincoln and Denzin, 1994, p.576).

The central characteristic of ethnographic research is that it asserts that all social action has meaning for those involved in it. If we want to understand others' behaviour (regardless of our own definition of this behaviour), then we must examine it from their perspective. Robson (1993) describes ethnography as:

> ... [seeking] to provide a written description of the implicit rules and traditions of a group. An ethnographer, through involvement with the group, tries to work out these rules. The intention is to provide a rich, or 'thick', description which interprets the experiences of people in the group from their own perspective.
>
> (Robson, 1993, p.148)

The involvement of ethnographers in the group being studied can be approached in a variety of ways. In *Understanding Everyday Life*, both **Redman's (2002)** and **Watson's (2002)** studies illustrate varied ethnographic research practices. A further case can be found in Chapter 6 of that volume (see **Jordan, 2002**), from Willmott and Young's (1957) now classic study of family and kinship networks in Bethnal Green, London. This used a range of quantitative and qualitative methods, including one of the researchers actually living in the area, with his children going to the local school.

All sociological research involves observation of varying types. However, there are limits to the number and kind of situations in which observation can take place in a less intrusive way, without it strongly affecting the situation being observed. As we noted earlier, the presence of another person always has an influence on the dynamics of the situation and observers can never fully assess the impact of their own presence. The nature of the disturbance depends on the topic and group being studied. It would be relatively straightforward, for example, to observe a football crowd from the outside. However, if one wished to observe and, more importantly, understand the behaviour of one particular group in that crowd, then it would most probably be necessary to become part of that group – to participate in it. In other words, one would need to become a **participant observation** 'participant observer'. **Participant observation** is an ethnographic method in which the researcher is part of a group whose activities they are, at the same time, observing. This method gives rise to some issues of concern, however. For example, how does the researcher join the group? How can they be a member of that group but at the same time remain sufficiently detached from the group to gather material? How can data be recorded? How does the researcher 'exit' the group? While a researcher's wider interests will influence the choice of group to study, it may well be that some of these difficulties may preclude, or make problematic, a particular piece of research.

3.1   Joining the group

One of the most important decisions for researchers when joining a group is whether to be overt – that is, to declare their true identity and aims – or to be covert and hide the fact that their aim is to carry out research. Sometimes, a middle way is taken, in which researchers provide some detail, but not the whole story. Diane Watson's participant observation was part of a wider ethnographic research project on a small chain of pubs. As she indicates in Chapter 5 of *Understanding Everyday Life* **(Watson, 2002)**, she spent many weeks, with another researcher, becoming involved in various aspects of the business. Because of this it was relatively easy for her to be seen as an insider by becoming a bar worker in a pub. The other bar staff knew of her background, but the customers did not. It is clear from her participant observation notes (see Reading 1.1 in Chapter 1 of this volume) that she managed to join the group, but for this she had to learn new behaviour. This meant that her entry into the group, at least as far as the customers were concerned, was relatively straightforward, unlike Whitehead's access to The Wagonner (see Reading 5.3 in Chapter 5 *Understanding Everyday Life*). Whitehead had lived for a number of years in the Herefordshire community where she was carrying out her research, and did not have particular problems with other pubs in the area. But she experienced difficulty gaining access to The Wagonner, which she describes as 'more exclusively a man's domain than any other [pub]', until her friendship with an 'insider' from the parish assisted her entry:

> The only unmarried woman who drank regularly at The Wagonner was the anthropologist. My class and stranger position, and my general eccentricity (by Herefordshire standards) made my first visits tolerable, but my access to the pub was only finally gained after one young married lorry driver whom I knew well pronounced the facilitating formula: 'Ann and me, we're like brother and sister. She's like a sister to me.'
>
> (Whitehead, 1976, p.176)

Consider now how much more difficult it might be if you were trying to gain entry to deviant or criminal groups. In Chapter 3 of *Understanding Everyday Life* Peter Hamilton talks of William Whyte's classic study of an Italian-American street gang in Chicago **(Hamilton, 2002)**. Whyte's entrée into the group resulted from his befriending the leader, 'Doc', and saying that he was a writer – truthful, but not the whole story. Whyte claims that this awareness of his intentions did have an effect on the gang's behaviour, and quotes Doc as saying: 'You've slowed me up plenty since you've been down here. Now, when I do something I would have to think that Bill Whyte would want to know about it and how to explain it. Before, I used to do things by instinct' (Whyte, 1981/1943, p.301).

On the other hand, when James Patrick (1973), a teacher in an approved school in Scotland, joined a juvenile gang in Glasgow, his true identity was known only to one person, Tim, who had facilitated his entry. They both agreed that, for their mutual safety, neither would reveal the true nature of Patrick's reasons for being in the gang. This is Patrick's account of his entry into the group:

> I was dressed in a mid-night blue suit, with a twelve-inch middle vent, three-inch flaps over the side pockets and a light blue handkerchief with a white polka dot (to match my tie) in the top pocket. My hair, which I had allowed to

grow long, was newly washed and combed into a parting just to the left of centre. My nails I had cut down as far as possible, leaving them ragged and dirty. I approached the gang of boys standing outside the pub and Tim, my contact, came forward to meet me, his cheeks red with embarrassment.

'Hello, sur, Ah never thoat ye wid come.'

Fortunately, the others had not heard the slip which almost ruined all my preparations.

I had not planned to join a juvenile gang; I had been invited. For two years I had been working in one of Scotland's approved schools during my vacations (as a student). During the Easter and Summer holidays of that year I had met Tim, who had been committed to the school some months previously. In discussion with the boys the topic of gangs and gang-warfare constantly cropped up. Tim … sidled up to me and asked me to come out with him and see for myself.

This combination of invitation and challenge worried me. … While I knew from records that Tim was a gang member, with an older brother serving a sentence for murder, the realisation of what an opportunity was being offered me … made me resolve to accept Tim's suggestion. … At first Tim thought that I should be introduced to his mates as an approved school teacher, but I soon pointed out the dangers and difficulties of that arrangement. For a start, I would then have been unlikely to see typical behaviour. It was slowly dawning on me that the best solution to the problem would be for me to become a participant observer. …

To overcome the problem of background, I decided to present myself as Tim's 'haufer' (i.e. his best friend in the approved school) who was out on leave at the same time, and, 'havin' nae people' had been befriended by Tim.

A third problem was that of language. Born and bred in Glasgow, I thought myself 'au fait' with the local dialect and after two years of part-time work with these boys I considered myself reasonably familiar with their slang – another serious mistake as it turned out. So confused was I on the first night that I had to 'play daft' to avoid too many questions and also to enable me to concentrate on what was being said.

After discussion with Tim I had bought the suit I have described in the first paragraph. Even here I made two mistakes. Firstly, I bought the suit outright with cash instead of 'paying it up' thus attracting both attention to myself in the shop and disbelief in the gang when I innocently mentioned the fact. Secondly, … I fastened the middle button of my jacket as I am accustomed to do. Tim was quick to spot the mistake. The boys in the gang fastened only the top button.

(Patrick, 1973, pp.13–14)

Patrick's entry into the juvenile Glasgow gang involved various challenges and required considerable preparation. While perhaps exceptional in the problems which he faced, his account illustrates some of the issues which need to be considered in this type of research. Ethical concerns are most relevant in this case and will be discussed later in this chapter. Group acceptance is a crucial stage in the ethnographic research process, but the collection and recording of the data also relate to important matters.

3.2 Collecting and recording the data

How easy do you think it would be to be involved in a group which you are observing and to maintain a 'professional distance' in order to observe and record your data? This depends, to a great extent, on the chosen topic and the location and on your personal 'fit' with the group. This is not easy in any situation, but it can be great fun and a very stimulating challenge. While there is an inherent conflict in the process of simultaneously participating and observing, training and strategic preparation can assist in productively managing this process.

ACTIVITY 3

Can you think of some of the difficulties that might arise when simultaneously being both observer and participant in a research situation? Think of Patrick's participation in a gang and/or Watson's in a pub, for example. Make a list of your answers.

You may have thought of some of the following:

- The difficulty of observing all of the behaviour around you, especially if your observation is in a busy place.
- Remembering what you have seen.
- Understanding and interpreting your observations and drawing conclusions from the behaviour you have observed.
- Making notes, especially if the group you are observing is unaware of your activity.
- The problem of learning new behaviour and meeting new people at the same time as trying to do your research, if you are in a relatively new situation.
- The ethics of covert observation.
- The influence of the researcher on the behaviour of others.
- Maintaining your relationship with others who know what your role is.
- The demands of a high level of involvement for the researcher over a long period of time.
- Gender, class and other personal differences which may influence both behaviour and its observation.
- Doing things you don't want to do, and do not agree with.

In Chapter 5 of *Understanding Everyday Life* Watson offers a good summary of what is required of the researcher in the dual role of participant and observer:

> For the researcher it is important to gain an understanding of the everyday events which are taking place. This involves both observing and describing what people are doing and a process of making inferences and interpretations. And this is all in addition to 'learning the ropes', coming to terms with an unfamiliar organizational setting and a new group of people, which, because of the difficulties of the task, is in danger of distracting the researcher completely. Obviously, everything that is observed or inferred has to be remembered until the researcher can find time and privacy to make notes. …
>
> …

If [the researcher acting as] the worker doesn't know the ropes, or understand the rules, then the performance is flawed and power shifts ... These power relationships are also gendered. The researcher is a woman and this is likely to influence the encounter ... These are established rules of engagement [of the field of research] ...

Ethical issues are raised by any participant observation but especially if the people don't know that they are being observed. It is often necessary for such research to be done covertly to be successful ... [But what] if [participants] discover later that the researcher ... was watching them with a different set of concerns in mind [?]. These are ethical matters, which have to be carefully considered beforehand if the research is not to be compromised.

(**Watson, 2002**, pp.211–12)

Watson's work involved some risk but was carried out in a generally acknowledged, non-threatening situation. Imagine, then, how much more difficult the process of participant observation must have been for James Patrick in his work with a violent Glasgow gang.

3.3   Exiting the group

Depending upon the situation the researcher finds themselves in, leaving the group they joined in order to conduct their research can be either relatively straightforward or fraught with difficulties. Watson's pub observation was, as she has said, part of a wider piece of ethnographic research, and lasted for a week. As the bar staff with whom she was working were aware of her academic background and the purpose of her working as a barmaid, leaving was not too difficult. Similarly, Anne Whitehead, in her study of pub activity in Herefordshire, had little problem in ending her observation. For James Patrick, however, the situation was somewhat different. He was very aware that his life, and his 'gatekeeper' Tim's, would be in danger if gang members became aware of his identity and Tim's collusion in the deception. Patrick experienced considerable personal violence from other gangs and from the police, which cemented his position within the gang, but decided to leave when he was expected to participate in ever-increasing violence. To do this he had to adopt a different identity and change job and geographical location – a high price to pay for a research project!

3.4   Further problems with ethnographic research

Ethnographic research is time consuming and can be expensive. It is labour intensive for the researcher and can often take several months, or even years, to generate the material sought. Some critics suggest that ethnographic material is unreliable since there is no way of checking the accuracy of either the data or the conclusions by replication. For example, it might be the case that the researcher becomes over-involved with the group being studied and some of the necessary detachment required by the research process is lost. It may also be that the very presence of another person might affect the behaviour of the group more than is realized. However, if the difficulties are acknowledged by the researcher and care is taken to be thorough and to avoid error, a considerable amount of rich and interesting data can be collected which would otherwise remain unknown. Yet, the purpose of collecting rich and interesting data is not simply to record the lives of different people, which might otherwise be inaccessible, but to consider the lived experience of selected individuals within the wider social world (Taylor, 2002). If we are to understand what social worlds are like from 'inside', and are to avoid imposing our own values on them, we will often need to rely on ethnographic methods.

SUMMARY OF SECTION 3

1   The central aim of the ethnographer is to provide a description of everyday life that is true to the particular group being studied.

2   Behaviour is observed in its own field setting with, as far as possible, minimal disruption from the researcher.

3   Ethnography acknowledges that all social action has meaning for those involved in it; therefore, if we want to understand others' behaviour, regardless of our own definition of it, we have to understand it from their perspective.

4   Ethnographic research provides rich in-depth data, which would be difficult, and often impossible, to generate in any other way.

---

4   Using documentary and visual material

Our discussion about qualitative interviewing and ethnographic studies has emphasized that qualitative data generation is concerned with observing and understanding social behaviour and the meanings which people give to that behaviour. We have noted that a range of research methods are included under the umbrella of qualitative research, and have so far considered aspects of qualitative interviewing and ethnography. Our focus in our discussion of interviewing has been mainly on semi-structured interviews, while under the umbrella of ethnography we have looked at participant observation. In this section we reflect on the use of documentary and visual material.

To study the meanings and practices of the social world, sociologists make use of the very practices they study, notably, as we have seen, conversations, audio-tape recordings, coding, observations and reflections. But they also use documentary and visual materials such as books, official historical records, diaries, autobiographies and letters, graphic representations, diagrams, scenes recorded on video tape and film, pictures, maps, and so on. Sociologists engage with these practices in a way similar to that in which we might highlight or annotate a text to draw out specific salient aspects or events in them.

Documents and visual material may be used as background to research or as research subjects in themselves. Ruth Finnegan (1996, pp.145–9) suggests a number of questions to ask that may guide the use of documentary – including visual – sources, thus allowing the researcher to assess the context of their production and their validity as research material. Such questions include:

1   What have the documents and visuals been used for and how far has account been taken of how and why they came into being?

2   Are the sources relevant and appropriate for the topic?

3   What kind of selection has been made in the use of sources and on what principles?

4   Has any account been taken of any 'twisting' or selection of the facts in the sources used?

5   How far does a particular source reflect a generality?

6   Is the source concerned with recommendations, ideals or what ought to be done?

7   How relevant is the context of the source?

8   With statistical sources, what were the assumptions underlying the original collection and presentation?

9   Has the meaning of the source been reasonably interpreted?

We shall address some of these questions with reference to examples of visual material. The most important point, however, for critically evaluating other people's research (and the use made of documentary evidence and visual materials) is whether the researcher has made clear the original source(s) of the data used, so that readers are able to check these.

In a textbook entitled *Visual Methodologies*, Gillian Rose (2001) notes that there is currently a lot of hype around 'the visual'. Considerable amounts of visual material have been produced in certain parts of the world, and there is confusion about how we should examine the visual through empirical studies and how the visual can best be studied and interpreted. There are few guides to this. Following Rose, we find that some of the best advice is Stuart Hall's:

> It is worth emphasizing that there is no single or 'correct' answer to the question, 'What does this image mean?' or 'What is this ad saying?' Since there is no law which can guarantee that things will have 'one, true, meaning', or that meanings won't change over time, work in this area is bound to be interpretative – a debate between, not who is 'right' and who is 'wrong', but between equally plausible, though sometimes competing and contesting, meanings and interpretations. The best way to 'settle' such contested reading is to look again at the concrete example and try to justify one's 'reading' in detail in relation to the actual practices and forms of signification [representation] used, and what meanings they seem to you to be producing.

(Hall, 1997, p.9)

To interpret an image you need to have an explicit methodology, since, as Hall suggests, you need to justify your interpretation. In this chapter we cannot enter into the wider debates about the visual and can only briefly address some of the issues of method involved in using visual materials. Quantitative methods can be deployed to interpret visual images (see, for example, Chapter 3 of Rose, 2001), and statistics are a form of documentary evidence, as we will discuss in Chapter 3 of this volume. But qualitative methods are generally seen as more appropriate for the interpretation of the visual. Our aim in this section is to highlight the importance of considering documents and the visual in terms of cultural significance, social practices and power relations.

One of the common uses of the visual in research is as documentary evidence, so in many ways these materials can be analysed by approaches similar to those used in analysing documents. But, as we noted above, to interpret these kinds of evidence we need to be aware that documentary material is not created in a vacuum, but informed by social context. Understanding this will enable you to develop an informed and critical awareness about research which uses these types of data.

In considering the use of visual (and other documentary) sources by writers and researchers, it is important to distinguish (as we do in more detail in Chapter 3) between 'primary' and 'secondary' sources. The definition of each is somewhat contentious. However, the general convention in the use of these types of data is that primary sources of documentary information are those that are produced by people directly involved with a given situation or study, and they therefore provide original raw data. A secondary source refers, in the context of documentary evidence, to information produced some time after the original event (as you will see in Chapter 3, secondary data can also refer to the use of material by people not directly involved with the study in which it was originally generated). Why is the distinction important, since it could be argued that 'the facts' are there and are indisputable? First, if only secondary sources are used, then the researcher has to take it on trust that what is claimed as factual is indeed accurate. Second, even when a source is factual, it may only present a partial story, and, if the topic is central to the research, this could lead to distorted and inaccurate results.

As we have already indicated, to elaborate on our discussion of issues of context in the use of documents in research, we are going to consider the case of visual material as documentary evidence. The key distinction between the analysis of visual material and other sorts of documents is that, if we wish to use visual material in research, we should start by acknowledging the power of the visual. The visual is very important in research – though researchers are not always aware of its power – and visual data can either be generated by the research process or be used to produce knowledge about particular issues. What we can see, how we see it, who secs it and who does not see it are questions to be used in the analysis of visual material.

If we invited you to identify some of the sources of visual evidence referred to in the Introduction to the book *Social Change* **(Jordan and Pile, 2002)** and in the first two chapters of that volume **(Pile, 2002; Bennett, 2002)**, you would no doubt have included in your list maps, photographs, pictures, diagrams, cartoons and posters. When we are faced with visual data, it is easy to forget that they are produced by a particular person or group of people for particular purposes. There is an interplay of agency and structure here – a decision has been made to present evidence in a certain way, but that decision is constrained by the accompanying circumstances. We rarely think about visual images as having been produced in context, but when we do, it becomes clear that the intention is to depict certain information in a particular visual manner. Similarly, when those images are used within the narrative of a textbook, for instance, the intention is to expand on what is being said, and to give a particular perspective on the data being presented. In order to illustrate the analysis of pictures, we will consider these issues in relation to two paintings from *Social Change* and how they were used by Tony Bennett in Chapter 2 of that volume. For example, look at the picture of 'Captain Cook Taking Possession of the Australian Continent on Behalf of the British Crown AD 1770', by Samuel Calvert. This is colour Plate 6 in *Social Change*.

Thinking back to Finnegan's points for assessing documentary evidence, which we listed above, you will note that:

- The picture is historical – both the uniforms and the ship indicate that it probably dates from around 200 years ago.
- It has something to do with Great Britain – the flag indicates that.
- It is on the seashore – ships and water can be seen.
- It relates to something official – the setting is formal and musicians are present.
- People other than soldiers also appear to be involved – one is holding a flag bearing a Union Jack.

We do not know a great deal more but we can make some inferences. From the title we know that it is a painting, dating back some 230 years or more, depicting the colonization of Australia by and for Britain. We cannot glean this information from the picture itself.

Next consider 'Possession Island' painted by Gordon Bennett in 1991. This is colour Plate 8 in *Social Change* and, like Plate 6, is also referred to by Tony Bennett in Chapter 2 of that volume. As Tony Bennett remarks, Gordon Bennett throws new light on the national narrative of Australia's foundation.

ACTIVITY 4

Now compare Plates 6 and 8 from *Social Change* and make a note of any differences between them that you spot.

You might have noted, among other things:

- Plate 8 depicts much the same scene as that depicted in Plate 6, but colonial relations are foregrounded by a different emphasis upon various elements.
- The background is less in focus.
- The black servant (scarcely noted in Calvert's painting in Plate 6) is dominant.
- Cook is less dominant but, taking off his hat, he appears to be more obvious.

What is the significance of these differences, and how can they be interpreted? The first things you might note are the flag and the setting. The Union Jack means (or denotes) 'Britishness' and here it is synonymous with the power of a colonist. The flag is prominently placed almost in the centre of the first picture. White men dominate, pictured larger than other figures, and appear to be in charge. Calvert's engraving of Cook reflects what Chapter 2 of *Social Change* calls Australia's 'monumental history', with Cook being depicted as the founding father of Australia. Tony Bennett remarks in Chapter 2 of *Social Change* that Cook's voyages and his exploits have been contested, in Aboriginal histories, as a Eurocentric mode of narrating the nation. Calvert's engraving, and particularly the flag, have engendered (or connoted) a feeling of pride and patriotism and a sense of history for many of Australia's white settlers from the UK. However, the feeling the picture connotes for Aboriginals (and for many others too) is one of piracy, power, control and subjugation – hence, the production of an alternative version by Gordon Bennett in 'Possession Island' where the foregrounding of the black servant negates the argument of *terra nullius* (or land that belongs to no one) and emphasizes the invasive nature of colonization. Here, then, the flag and the picture denote a particular occasion, but *connote* a very different interpretation of that occasion, depending upon the perspective of the viewer.

To interpret the use that was made of this material in Chapter 2 of *Social Change*, we need to ask what was in the author's mind when he chose these particular pictures. What have they been used for and how far has the author taken account of them? Are the sources relevant and appropriate for the research topic? What kind of selection has been made in the use of the sources and on what principles? Has the meaning of the source been reasonably interpreted? These questions refer to the ways of interpreting documentary sources (of which the visual is a part), discussed by Finnegan (1996) and referred to earlier. Let us consider the questions closely, under two broad topics: (1) use and interpretation, and (2) assessment in relation to claims in the narrative.

1   *Use and interpretation.* What has Tony Bennett used the pictures for and how far has he taken account of how and why they came into being? Has the meaning of the source been reasonably interpreted? When you read Chapter 2 of *Social Change*, particularly section 5 on critical histories, you saw that the author used the pictures to illustrate his argument about what was the officially accepted approach to the history of Australia, and how that has changed due to resistance from the indigenous population. Bennett uses the term 'critical' in relation to history, in the sense of challenging prevailing historical texts from the alternative perspective of the Aborigines. His use of Calvert's picture reflects the (hi)story of Australia, told from the perspective of the dominant white settlers finding a new and 'uninhabited' country. He then goes on to juxtapose this picture with that of Gordon Bennett, to give an alternative, critical, version of the colonization of Australia. Tony Bennett is using the pictures as a graphic illustration of the changing history of Australia. The pictures not only support the narrative in the chapter, but they are also supported by other historical sources, both in Australia and in the UK. Clearly then, they are located directly in the different interpretations of history which the author has discussed.

2   *Are the sources relevant and appropriate for the research topic? How relevant is the context of the source?* The original context of the sources – reflecting the claiming of Australia for Britain and the reinterpretation of that by an Aboriginal artist – is clearly in line with Tony Bennett's narrative. You could ask the question, though, why are they there? Would their removal detract from what is being said? You could argue that they add another dimension and perspective to the narrative. The visual images reinforce, reflect and consolidate what has been discussed in the narrative, and give you, the student, a much broader and richer picture. The important thing to remember, however, is that visual images like these are rarely used on their own – some setting is generally needed within which to locate them. What you need to bear in mind is that selectivity has occurred and the selection of a different set of pictures may well have told a different (hi)story.

SUMMARY OF SECTION 4

1   Documentary material and visual images are always constructed in context, with varying intentions and using various practices, technologies and knowledge.

2   Documentary and visual materials have a variety of uses. They are often deployed as illustration but can be a vital part of evidence collected in qualitative research.

3   For the critical reading and interpretation of documents and of visual material, it is important to be aware of the context within which they were created, as well as the way they have been used by the writer/researcher.

4   A critical approach to visual images needs to consider the agency of the image, the social practices and effects of their viewing, and the specificity of that viewing for any particular audience (for example, an audience of students of DD201 *Sociology and Society*).

5   Doing ethical research

A concern with ethics should pervade the whole research process, from the original research design, the techniques of data generation, the data management procedures, to the presentation of data. From the Greek word *ethos*, which means character, ethics is the systematic study of values, such as 'good', 'bad', 'right' and 'wrong', and the general principles which underlie these concepts. In general, ethics in research concerns the morality of the way in which data are collected and used. Ethical research recognizes possible power imbalances between the participants in a study – the researcher and those being researched – and attempts to create a mutually beneficial situation in which people are more likely to act openly and honestly. This is common sense, but perceiving common sense is not always straightforward. It could be easier for a researcher to focus narrowly on completing a research project (especially if working under time, financial and organizational constraints), and to overlook or even ignore the interests and perspectives of both the participants and the wider society. Researchers may consider that the important thing is to 'get the data', and may ignore the needs of the participants. Yet, participants have power and agency and may respond with avoidance, lies and subterfuge regardless of the methods used to gain data – people can lie in an open interview just as they can lie on a standard closed questionnaire. Ramazanoglu elaborates this point in a discussion of her research with women shift-workers:

> The women generally saw the interview situation as an unequal one in which I had control. They resisted this through defensive attitudes to questioning and also by offering me cigarettes or sweets which slightly altered the balance of the interview. There was no way that good interview rapport or a trusting relationship could be established when I was identified in this way … The women had good reason to be cautious as I did not question the assumption that the survey results would be available to management, and could be used to control women's lives.
>
> (Ramazanoglu, 1989, p.431)

Certain ethical principles should be followed to guide good research practice. For Sieber (1992) these are:

1   *Beneficence*, which means maximizing good outcomes for all the research participants.

2   *Respect*, which means protecting individual autonomy – whether participants are autonomous or whether they may need help in decision making (for example, people with learning difficulties and children). This also involves acknowledging the individual's right not to respond to a question, or to withdraw permission for the use of certain information. This can be quite frustrating if time and energy have been used to collect the data. However, withdrawal of permission is rarely a problem, providing the right ethical principles have been adopted from the start.

3   *Justice*, which signifies ensuring fair distribution of costs and benefits among persons and groups, so that those who bear the risks of research should be those who benefit the most from it.

These three principles entail identifying the consequences of research and ensuring that the individuals involved are fully aware of what is happening before they give their consent. This involves an assessment of risks and benefits. Ethical research will respect privacy, maximize benefit and minimize risk.

How can these principles be worked out in actual research practice? The British Sociological Association's charter of ethics, for example, outlines that 'Sociologists, when they carry out research, enter into personal and moral relationships with those they study, be they individuals, households, social groups or corporate entities' (British Sociological Association, 2002, item 10). Yet, the relationship between researchers and the people they study in certain areas is not easy and straightforward, with many factors needing to be taken into consideration. You may think of the example of covert ethnographic research discussed earlier. In such circumstances the way in which research ethics are handled will, in large part, be influenced by the theoretical approach of the research project. Four basic ethical questions seem relevant to this discussion:

1   What is the impact of informed consent on the ability to obtain high-quality data, and what constitutes 'informed consent'?

2   How does an investigator become sensitive to and respectful of what is 'private' or 'dangerous' to subjects?

3   What promises of confidentiality and anonymity should and should not be made? How can the investigator assure the confidentiality that is promised? How do consent, confidentiality and anonymity influence the kinds of information subjects are willing to provide to researchers?

4   When, if ever, is the use of deception acceptable?

ACTIVITY 5

What do you think the concept of 'voluntary informed consent' might involve? Make some notes on your ideas.

Home
- How to contact us
- Media and Research enquiries
- Useful Documents
- What the BSA is doing for Sociologists

Introducing Sociology
- About the BSA
- What is sociology?
- What do sociologists do?
- How is Sociological Research Conducted?
- Opportunities for Sociologists
- Where to Study Sociology
- Sociology Links

Organisation of the BSA
- Organisation of the BSA
- Executive Committee
- Sub-Committees
- BSA Office
- Forums
- Task Groups

Professional Standards
- Authorship Guidelines
- Good Professional Conduct
- Statement of Ethical Practice
- Anti-Sexist Language
- Anti-Racist Language
- Ablist and Non-Disablist Language
- Employment of Staff
- Applications for Research Funding
- Dealing with Sexual Harassment
- Postgraduate Research In Sociology

Prizes
- Prizes
- Philip Abrams Book Prize
- Phil Strong Memorial Prizes
- Sociology of Health and Illness Book of the Year

About the BSA
Giving Sociology a Voice

STATEMENT OF ETHICAL PRACTICE FOR THE BRITISH
SOCIOLOGICAL ASSOCIATION
MARCH 2002

Click Here to download the Statement of Ethical Practice

Statement of Ethical Practice

This statement is one of a set of Guidelines on a variety of fundamental aspects of professional sociology.

The British Sociological Association gratefully acknowledges the use made of the ethical codes and statements of the Social Research Association, the American Sociological Association and the Association of Social Anthropologists of the UK and the Commonwealth

1) The purpose of the statement is to make members aware of the ethical issues that may arise throughout the research process and to encourage them to take responsibility for their own ethical practice. The Association encourages members to use the Statement to help educate themselves and their colleagues to behave ethically.

2) The statement does not, therefore, provide a set of recipes for resolving ethical choices or dilemmas, but recognises that it will be necessary to make such choices on the basis of principles and values, and the (often conflicting) interests of those involved.

3) Styles of sociological work are diverse and subject to change, not least because sociologists work within a wide variety of settings. Sociologists, in carrying out their work, inevitably face ethical, and sometimes legal, dilemmas which arise out of competing obligations and conflicts of interest.

4) The following statement advises members of the Association about ethical concerns and potential problems and conflicts of interest that may arise in the course of their professional activities. The statement is not exhaustive but summarises basic principles for ethical practice by sociologists. Departures from the principles should be the result of deliberation and not ignorance.

Figure 2.3   *Extract from 'Statement of ethical practice for the British Sociological Association' (March 2002). The full statement can be found on the British Sociological Association's website: www.britsoc.co.uk*

You may have noted that *voluntary informed consent* might involve participating willingly without coercion, being told what the research is about, and agreeing to be part of the research. If so, you are quite right, but it is helpful to clarify and expand on what this involves.

- Informed consent should be obtained before the relevant part of the research process begins and should, as implied by the question in Activity 5, be voluntary. Voluntary means given *freely*, without undue threat or enticement. *Informed consent* requires a clear, simple explanation which participants will understand. It is best to avoid technical language. Although one could argue that participation is clearly indicative of consent having been given, this should not be regarded as a 'once-and-for-all' agreement. Consent is an ongoing, two-way process between the researcher and those from whom the data are 'collected'. The participant should be given the opportunity to ask questions and to refuse to participate.

- Similarly, the people from whom data are collected must be treated with respect and be able to feel that they can trust the researcher. Securing formal consent is important to this process, but other things – such as body language, friendliness, a respectful attitude and genuine empathy for the role of the subject – may speak louder than words.

- For instance, *consent* does not necessarily have to be written provided that a clear explanation has been given, and there is understanding and empathy between participant and researcher. Indeed, participation may be taken as tacit agreement and, in some cases, signed agreements may be detrimental to the research participant, as, for example, in the case of criminal behaviour.

- It is also important that enough time is given for consideration of participation, particularly when interviewing. This is very relevant when asking for volunteers from a group. Group pressure may lead to individuals volunteering to participate in research when they have no intention of doing so, or second thoughts may lead them to change their initial decision. Either way, there is a need to recognize this possibility and to have a contingency plan to fall back on.

The ethical concerns of the relationship between researcher and participants do not stop once the research is over. In many cases it is important to allow time for contact following the interview to discuss the topic in general, or any specific issues that the interview may have raised for individuals. This is particularly important when discussing sensitive topics, and interviewees may well reflect on and decide that they have given information that they would rather the researcher did not use. (Issues arising from doing research in sensitive areas are explored more fully in the audio-visual material accompanying this module.)

Further important ethical issues to consider include those related to privacy, confidentiality and anonymity. *Privacy* refers to individuals and *their* control of our access to information about them. We certainly know when our own privacy has been invaded – but we need to recognize that this feeling is likely to differ from person to person. How do researchers know when someone participating in their study is likely to feel invaded? Sensitivity to body language and verbal responses will give clues, and someone's clear reluctance or hesitation in answering a question may indicate their feelings of vulnerability. However, it is not just the question being asked with which participants will be concerned, but also with what is going to be done with the interview material afterwards. If researchers are not sensitive to these issues, then the evasions or even lies which subjects may use to guard their privacy will call into question the integrity of the research.

Confidentiality concerns data about individuals and who should or should not have access to these data, as we mentioned earlier in our discussion about qualitative interviews. Ideally, issues of confidentiality will be sorted out as part of an informed consent agreement. This raises a complex ethical issue. Given that the reason for collecting the material in the first place is to disseminate it, albeit in a different format, *one cannot offer complete confidentiality*. The important point here is that the individual should not be identified by the material they have given, and that the researcher will take measures to ensure that the raw data are not available for general perusal. This, then, links confidentiality with anonymity.

Anonymity means safeguarding the identity of the participants. It means separating the data from any way in which the participant might be identified. The issue of anonymity is particularly difficult when it is important to have certain data for analysis or follow-up. However, a system of coding can be used, where the codes and the data are kept totally separate and under secure conditions. Researchers can use numbers to identify respondents, but there is a preference for the use of pseudonyms which make the data more 'human'. This was done by **Redman (2002)**. **Watson (2002)** anonymized some participants but clearly identified (by name and appearance) others, as not everyone felt the need to be anonymous. What can be easily overlooked, though, is identification by means other than name or appearance. This is a particular problem for insider-researchers within organizations where people can be recognized by their position in the establishment. Protecting the identity of these individuals may well require further ingenuity. On the other hand, it could also happen that participants may wish to be identified as a means of advertising themselves (their skills or services, for example), and this should be carefully considered.

As well as ethical issues, any researcher, whether new or experienced, has to be aware of legal requirements in relation to data. For example, in the UK the Data Protection Act 1998 controls the use of personal information that has been collected. Researchers must make themselves aware of the legal context in which they operate. This includes the implications of using deception.

Although deception is essential for the study of some kinds of behaviour, there are serious concerns about and objections to its use. Deception in research may result in an invasion of privacy, it may reduce individual autonomy, and could cause a generalized suspicion of research and researchers. However, there are at least three defensible justifications for the use of deception (see also Sieber, 1992, p.94):

1   Where participants' behaviour would otherwise change to such a degree as to render the research worthless (though *post hoc* consent should normally be obtained in such circumstances).

2   Where participants may be put at serious risk if the researcher's identity or the purpose of the research were known. For example, research collaborators can sometimes face the threat of reprisal if it becomes known that they have facilitated the entry of a researcher – this may be the case when researching criminal activity, for instance.

3   Where there is a strong case to be made that deception is for the 'public good' (for example, when researching corporate corruption or dangerous individuals or groups).

In this context, it might be worth revisiting James Patrick's ethnographic research which we discussed earlier (similar issues are raised in the discussion of David Calvey's research on nightclub bouncers, in the audio-visual material accompanying this module). As you will recall, Patrick joined a delinquent Glasgow gang under cover and observed the gang's activities. What do you think the ethical issues involved in his conduct were?

- The researcher certainly put his own life at risk, as well as that of his gatekeeper, Tim. However, Tim apparently knew better than Patrick what the risks were. It could be argued that Tim gave some sort of consent to be involved in the research.

- What of the criminal activities in which the gang were involved? Although not entirely clear from the extract itself, Patrick in fact managed to be involved only on the margins, often acting as 'look-out' and keeping out of some of the more serious criminal activities.

- However, it could be argued that, by participating, Patrick was ignoring the criminal behaviour of the group and compromising his own values as a reform school teacher. Indeed, in the end, with the stabbing of a member of another gang, Patrick's values were compromised too much, and he left the group.

We can now return to the question: was Patrick's action justified in collecting data which could not have been collected in any other way? As David Calvey's (1999) research also makes clear, these are not easy issues to resolve, but ultimately a researcher's key responsibility in most circumstances is to the well-being of those whom they are researching. Exceptional circumstances – such as when researching powerful or dangerous groups or individuals – may violate this rule, and will need to be assessed on their own merit, but in general terms it will hold true.

    In more specific terms, however, researchers may need to draw on other resources to judge the ethical principles of their conduct. While ethical guidelines from professional bodies are valuable in assisting researchers in ethical conduct, they are not always appropriate to the circumstances of the study. In this regard, Hollway and Jefferson (2000, pp.110–2) found that, when approaching research within a framework requiring the understanding of the interdependency between researcher and participant, the key basis for an ethical relationship is to pursue the values of honesty, sympathy and respect, from the personal relationship to the analysis of the research material. Honesty relates to the integrity of the analysis in situations where evidence is not just ignored when it does not suit, and judgements are based on evidence, within a theoretical framework that is justified and clearly laid out. Sympathy implies putting one's self-knowledge and one's familiarity with difficulties to assist the understanding of interviewees' points of view. Respect involves bringing to the study all forms of knowledge at one's disposal – theoretical, empirical and experiential – and looking at the data through the lens of all these various knowledges, in order to notice what is normally overlooked or might be too painful to notice. Hollway and Jefferson's (2000) views refine the principles outlined by Sieber (1992) and mentioned above.

Thus, we can see that ethics is concerned with protecting the privacy of the subject, and creating a situation that benefits both researcher and researched. The crux of the whole issue is to assess the risks and benefits – to the participant, to the researcher, to sociological knowledge, to any organization that may be involved, and to future research. A final cautionary point is that such a risk assessment is not easy.

Ethical concerns are relevant for the conduct of any sort of research practice in which the sociologist may be involved. At the end of the research process the researcher needs to convince themselves and others that the explanation they have constructed and the material they have assembled are reliable and accurate, that the data generated are valid and that the research can describe a situation in a particular or general way. In concluding this chapter we recapitulate the various phases of the research process and address the questions of validity and generalization.

SUMMARY OF SECTION 5

1   Some risks and benefits cannot be assessed accurately before the investigation is carried out.

2   Some benefits may be long-term and not immediately visible.

3   One participant's risk may be another participant's benefit.

4   It is critical for the research process to understand participants properly and this is perhaps best guaranteed when researchers pursue honesty, sympathy and respect in their work.

---

6   Validity and generalizability in qualitative research

As you have seen in the course of this chapter, qualitative research is concerned with how the world is interpreted – that is, it is concerned with understanding both the experience and the production of the social world. As you have also seen, the methods used to generate qualitative data are contextually sensitive and flexible, and involve understanding the context itself and the complexity and detail present in this context. In the act of qualitative research the researcher moves back and forth as the investigation progresses, dealing with more than one element of the research process at a time. Yet, the phases of research are distinct, each requiring particular skills.

Research often starts with the identification of a broad topic or area of exploration. The planning and designing of the study follows. The importance of a research plan – or design – lies in enabling the researcher to consider all the steps and issues involved in the investigation, offering a coherent basis upon which to proceed. The planning and designing of a research project is not peculiar to qualitative research – the same steps are involved in quantitative approaches. However, the potential for flexible changes in the original project is greater, and usually less costly, in qualitative approaches. The processes of generating qualitative material are linked to an original plan, but also include questioning the theoretical context throughout the investigation. We have explored these processes in this chapter by means of interviewing, ethnographic observation, and the use of documents and visual materials. We referred to sampling and to the selection of individuals and cases. We noted how sampling in qualitative research is usually theoretically driven, and we will discuss sampling strategies further in the next chapter. This is an area of the research that, although defined in the original plan, can be changed as the investigation progresses and further issues in need of exploration come to light. The sorting, organizing and coding of material is a process informed by the original questions, plan and design, and is a phase that follows immediately from the gathering of material from the 'field'. We have noted that this is not a discrete phase, since the various classifications of material may correspond to the exploration of particular research questions, some of which may emerge in the very process of analysis. At the end of this whole process, convincing explanations and analyses are expected to emerge. This is when the analytical thoughts from the project, the original research design, research questions and the broad topic of investigation are linked up. What is it that we want to know? How can our material relate to what we have sought to explore? At this point we need to demonstrate that our analysis is accurate or *valid*.

As we noted when discussing semi-structured interviewing (see section 2.1 above), for positivists, the authority of a particular finding is in part derived from the ability to replicate or reproduce it. However, in qualitative research this is problematic, since qualitative research methods are designed to respond to what is specific and contextual to a given phenomenon or interaction (for instance, qualitative interviewers adapt their questions in order to maximize interviewees' ability to speak from their own perspective or from 'within their own social world'). This lack of standardization in qualitative methods means that qualitative data are often difficult to replicate. In consequence, the common way to assess whether we are 'measuring' – or 'capturing' – what we claim to be measuring when using qualitative research methods, is by means of judgements concerning **validity**.   **validity**

Mason (1996) suggests that validity of method and analysis should be demonstrated in two ways. The first refers to *validity of data-generation methods* and involves asking how well the data sources and methods can be used for an adequate social explanation. You may want to argue why a particular document is authentic, accurate or relevant. You may wish to regard data generated from some interviews as more valid for your research questions than data generated from other interviews. Explaining how you came to the conclusion that your choices and methods were valid is usually the best way of demonstrating the validity of your claims.

The second way of demonstrating the validity of a study is by means of *validity of interpretation*. This can be achieved by making transparent how it is that you have arrived at a particular interpretation. Your interpretation cannot be valid unless your methods and sources enable you to elaborate upon the explanations you seek. You need to make a case for why your audience should accept your interpretation over alternative ones, and why they should believe that you have not misinterpreted the material. A careful retracing of the route taken in the investigation is thus often needed to demonstrate validity.

The investigation often carries greater validity when it resonates with wider contexts, and this raises the question of how far the results of qualitative research can be *generalized* – that is, extrapolated to a larger population. The understanding of your own research strategy, and in particular the relationship between your sample (of individuals and materials) and the broader empirical and theoretical connections in the field of sociology, is crucial to support generalization claims. In the polarized debates between qualitative and quantitative research, quantitative methods are often said to generate knowledge of the social world in breadth while qualitative methods are often said to generate knowledge in depth. But, as Hollway and Jefferson (2000) have convincingly argued, the study of individual cases is a reminder that generalizations that do not take into account biographical, as well as demographic, data are unlikely to prove very useful. In other words, it is possible for accounts to be so generalized that they apply to nothing or no one in particular. For this reason, Hollway and Jefferson advocate combining methods to generate accounts in both depth and breadth. Yet, as we will argue in the next chapter, the combination of different research methods needs careful consideration, and the use of more than one method may create further problems of validity as different methods are assessed. However, it remains the case that multiple methods can reveal a more complex social reality and enhance validity if properly deployed.

To make generalized claims it is important to ask yourself certain questions, as suggested by Mason (1996, pp.156–7):

■ 'What kinds of generalization do my *research questions* imply?' (p.156)

■ 'What kinds of generalization does my *sampling strategy* support?' (p.157)

■ 'What kinds of generalization do my *methods of sorting and organizing data* support?' (p.157)

These questions allow you to review the whole research process and to be clear about the sorts of generalizations you want to, and are able to, make. They also help you to understand how the generalizations are supported by all the elements of your research design and practice, from beginning to end. However, it is important to remember that generalization is not easy to achieve in any research, not just in qualitative research.

SUMMARY OF SECTION 6

1   Validity refers to the extent to which research successfully captures the reality of the phenomenon under study.

2   It can be assessed in relation to the validity of data generation methods and validity of interpretation.

3   Qualitative methods are often said to generate knowledge in depth – that is, knowledge about the local, contextual and particular. However, they can sometimes be used to make generalized claims that can be applied to wider populations or contexts.

4   Where generalized claims are made, researchers need to ensure they can support these in relation to their research questions, their sampling strategies and their methods of organizing their data.

7   Conclusion

A final reminder of the strengths and weaknesses of qualitative approaches is in order here, bearing in mind that the core strength of qualitative research rests on the competence with which the analysis is carried out. On the other hand, the central weakness of qualitative studies is their potential mismanagement due to poor research training of those developing them. Qualitative methods demand a lot of close involvement on the part of researchers if they are to produce studies that make a significant sociological contribution.

Strengths of qualitative sociological research

1   Qualitative research focuses on events that occur naturally and ordinarily in 'natural' settings, allowing researchers to have a strong handle on what 'real life' is like.

2   Data are collected in close proximity to the actual situation and are focused on phenomena occurring within particular boundaries and embedded in context.

3   The social context is taken into account in understanding the situation.

4   Data reveal complexity and allow for further issues to be included as the investigation proceeds.

5   Qualitative research enables flexibility: times and methods of generating data can vary as the study progresses, maximizing the potential for researchers to understand the social world in question.

6   With its emphasis on people's lived experiences, qualitative research is well suited to locating meanings that are placed on the events, processes and structures of people's lives; their perceptions, assumptions and presuppositions; and for connecting these to the social world.

Weaknesses of qualitative sociological research

1   Qualitative research relies strongly on the skills and ability of researchers to establish connections between the various elements of the situation being studied and the social context in which it is embedded.

2   An enormous amount of data is often generated, requiring close and expert management to avoid waste and potentially wrong interpretation.

3   The process of discovery can be messy if procedures to connect theoretical and empirical material are not pursued throughout the investigation.

4   Data may reveal particularities that have little value beyond the particular situation explored.

5   The production of robust claims on the basis of qualitative methods demands considerable effort and skills to generate appropriate validity and generalizability from the data.

References

Bennett, T. (2002) 'Contesting times: conflicting histories in post-colonial contexts' in Jordan, T. and Pile, S. (eds) *op. cit.*

Bennett, T. and Watson, D. (eds) (2002a) *Understanding Everyday Life*, **Oxford, Blackwell/The Open University.**

Bennett, T. and Watson, D. (2002b) 'Understanding everyday life: introduction' in Bennett, T. and Watson, D. (eds) *op. cit.*

British Sociological Association (2002) *Ethics Guidelines*, Durham, British Sociological Association.

Burgess, R. (1984) *Field Research: A Sourcebook and Field Manual*, London, Unwin Hyman.

Calvey, D. (1999) 'Getting on the door and staying in there: a covert participant observational study of bouncers' in Lee-Treweek, G. and Linkogle, S. (eds) *Danger in the Field*, London, Routledge.

Denzin, N.K. and Lincoln, Y.S. (1994) *Handbook of Qualitative Research*, London, Sage.

Epstein, D. and Johnson, R. (1998) *Schooling Sexualities*, Buckingham, Open University Press.

Finnegan, R. (1996) 'Using documents' in Sapsford, R. and Jupp, V. (eds) *Data Collection and Analysis*, London, Sage.

Flick, U. (1998) *An Introduction to Qualitative Research*, London, Sage.

Hall, S. (1997) 'Introduction' in Hall, S. (ed.) *Representation: Cultural Representations and Signifying Practices*, London, Sage/The Open University.

Hamilton, P. (2002) 'The street and everyday life' in Bennett, T. and Watson, D. (eds) *op. cit.*

Hammersley, M. and Atkinson, P. (1990) *Ethnography: Principles in Practice* (2nd edn), London, Routledge.

Hemmings, S., Silva, E.B. and Thompson, K. (2002) 'Accounting for the everyday' in Bennett, T. and Watson, D. (eds) *op. cit.*

Hollway, W. and Jefferson, T. (2000) *Doing Qualitative Research Differently*, London, Sage.

Jordan, T. (2002) 'Community, everyday and space' in Bennett, T. and Watson, D. (eds) *op. cit.*

Jordan, T. and Pile, S. (2002) *Social Change*, **Oxford, Blackwell/The Open University.**

Lincoln Y.S. and Denzin, N.K. (1994) 'The fifth moment' in Denzin, N.K. and Lincoln, Y.S. (eds) *op. cit.*

Mason, J. (1996) *Qualitative Researching*, London, Sage.

Oakley, A. (2002) *Experiments in Knowing. Gender and Method in the Social Sciences*, Cambridge, Polity Press.

Patrick, J. (1973) *A Glasgow Gang Observed*, London, Eyre Methuen.

Payne, G., Williams, M. and Chamberlain, S. (2004) 'Methodological pluralism in British Sociology', *Sociology*, vol.38, no.1, pp.153–64.

Pile, S. (2002) 'Social change and city life' in Jordan, T. and Pile, S. (eds) *op. cit.*

Ramazanoglu, C. (1989) 'Improving our sociology: the problems of taking a feminist standpoint', *Sociology*, vol.23, no.3, pp.427–42.

Redman, P. (1999) 'Boys in love: narrative, identity and the production of heterosexual masculinities', unpublished PhD thesis, University of Birmingham.

Redman, P. (2002) 'Love is in the air: romance and the everyday' in Bennett, T. and Watson, D. (eds) *op. cit*.

Robson, C. (1993) *Real World Research*, Oxford, Blackwell.

Rogers, C.R. (1944) 'The non-directive methods: a technique for social research', *American Journal of Sociology*, no.50, pp.279–93.

Rose, G. (2001) *Visual Methodologies*, London, Sage.

Sieber, J. (1992) *Planning Ethically Responsible Research*, Applied Social Research Methods Series Volume 31, London, Sage.

Silva, E.B. (1988) 'Labour and technology in the car industry. Ford strategies in Britain and Brazil', unpublished PhD thesis, University of London.

Silva, E.B. (2004) 'Notes on fieldwork' (mimeo), *Cultural Capital and Social Exclusion Project*, Milton Keynes, The Open University Sociology Discipline.

Taylor, S. (ed.) (2002) *Ethnographic Research. A Reader*, London, Sage.

Watson, D. (2002) '"Home from home": the pub and everyday life' in Bennett, T. and Watson, D. (eds) *op. cit.*

Whitehead, A. (1976) 'Sexual antagonism in Hertfordshire' in Barker, D. and Allen, S. (eds) *Dependence and Exploitation in Work and Marriage*, London, Longman.

Whyte, W.F. (1981) 'The gang and the individual' in Whyte, W.F. *Street Corner Society: The Social Structure of an Italian Slum* (3rd edn), Chicago, IL, University of Chicago Press. (First published in 1943.)

Willmott, P. and Young, M. (1957) *Family and Kinship in East London*, London, Routledge & Kegan Paul.

Quantitative sociological research

Janet Parr and Elizabeth B. Silva

Contents

1 Introduction

From your reading of Chapters 1 and 2 of this volume, you will recognize that quantitative and qualitative methods are often seen as being fundamentally different – indeed, as embodying opposing positivist and interpretivist views about the nature of the social world and how we can best have knowledge of this. Needless to say, there are good reasons why positivist sociologists have often chosen to adopt quantitative methods, just as there are good reasons why interpretivist sociologists have often chosen to adopt qualitative methods. However, as Chapters 1 and 2 also sought to argue, we should not assume that a particular research method (whether quantitative or qualitative) must always and of necessity be connected to a particular epistemological or ontological position. Quantitative research methods, although often associated with the positivist tradition, are not *inherently* positivist and, by the same token, qualitative research methods, though often associated with interpretivism, are not *inherently* interpretivist.

This argument – that quantitative research methods are not inherently positivist – is the starting-point for this chapter, for it allows us to approach quantitative research as a fundamentally social product: the outcome of practices, concepts, instruments, orientations and uses that demand to be seen in social terms. Indeed, viewed in this light, quantitative methods have rather more in common with qualitative methods than is often claimed since both can be understood as necessarily involving the production of knowledge in a social context.

This is not how quantitative methods have been conventionally understood. Quantitative research has been widely seen as a form of knowledge untainted by social values, while the status of numerical evidence as factual and objective has allowed it to be portrayed as an asocial product untouched by human hand. Quantitative researchers are commonly viewed as clinically collecting and preserving the 'facts', where facts are taken as things that are there to be collected. Yet, as we saw in Chapter 1, sociological research cannot easily imitate research in the natural sciences because it is more difficult for the sociological researcher to be a 'detached observer'. The 'subject–object problem' referred to in section 4.1 of Chapter 1, means that it must not be assumed that sociological researchers can be protected from involvement with the object of their study.

The clear implication of this is that quantitative methods are no more theory or value free than qualitative approaches. Thus, most of the concerns raised in the last chapter, about the ways in which data generation is embedded in the social, apply equally to reflections on the production of knowledge using quantification techniques. Irvine *et al.* (1979) provide a useful summary of this argument, drawing our attention to four major respects in which quantitative research needs to be understood in social terms. They argue that:

1   Quantitative data should be viewed as *historically located* or situated. This is because knowledge is always produced within and shaped by human activities, choices and conflicts. Quantitative data are not, therefore, neutral or objective but need to be evaluated in this light.

2   All data – whether quantitative or otherwise – are structured by a *conceptual framework* as well as by the technical instruments used in their production. We therefore need to investigate the nature of these theoretical and practical choices for the data in question.

3   Official data – or statistics – are *particular social products*, which reflect the administrative and political practices of government and state. It is important to know how and why certain statistics are produced in specific ways and why data on some important social issues are not available.

4   Quantitative analyses have often underpinned supposedly rational decision making, providing a basis for all-purpose scientific and technical solutions to various kinds of problems. Such solutions are regarded as disinterested and neutral, but they are actually *interested* and *predisposed.*

To explore these issues, in sections 2, 3 and 4 of this chapter we examine the implications of considering quantitative research as social knowledge. We do this in relation to engagement with two forms of data and their analysis and presentation. In section 2 we look at secondary quantitative data, drawing on examples you will already have met in your reading of *Social Differences and Divisions* **(Braham and Janes, 2002)**, and on official census material. In section 3 we consider primary quantitative data – as produced by social surveys, for example. We move on in section 4 to consider the analysis and presentation of these data. Sections 3 and 4 are organized slightly differently from most chapters in the DD201 course books in that they are structured, in part, around an exercise to create and analyse a research questionnaire. Section 5 concludes the chapter by reconsidering the epistemological assumptions of quantitative research, as well as the issue of ethics. At this point the chapter returns to the traditional assumptions of quantification, comparing them with the understanding of quantitative research as social knowledge.

AIMS

The aims of this chapter are:

1   To consider quantitative research as a form of social knowledge.

2   To discuss the implications of using secondary quantitative data.

3   To examine the production of primary quantitative data.

4   To reconsider, in relation to the discussion in the previous chapter, the implications of epistemological assumptions for the production of knowledge, and the issue of ethics, in relation to quantitative approaches to sociological research.

---

2   Quantitative research as social knowledge (1): engaging with secondary data

The scale of quantitative research varies from large surveys to small number counting (that is, small-scale numerical evidence). Examples of these practices can be found throughout DD201, but a good number of both appear in *Social Differences and Divisions* **(Braham and Janes, 2002)**. For instance, in Chapter 1, Linda Janes and Gerry Mooney refer to geodemographic classification systems and a survey on health, both of which comprise extensive data sets **(Janes and Mooney, 2002)**. Similarly, in Chapter 2, Mike Savage refers to social surveys on attitudes and class consciousness **(Savage, 2002)**; in Chapter 3, Linda Janes uses data from the British Social Attitudes Survey **(Janes, 2002)**. On a much

Figure 3.1 *'National Statistics Online' (http://www.statistics.gov.uk/), one of the websites of the UK's Office for National Statistics, provides an extensive source of secondary statistical data*

smaller scale, the numerical data on the gated communities discussed in Chapter 1 of that volume refer to particular geographical areas, while selected social groups are the main concern of Chapter 3. In the rest of this section, we look at some of these examples in more detail, concentrating mainly on issues regarding census data and large official surveys, presented in the form of statistics.

The Pocket Oxford Dictionary (2002) defines statistics as 'numerical facts systematically collected on a subject', understanding facts to be 'things known to be true'. Thus conceived, a statistician is an expert in numerical things known to be true, systematically collected on a subject. However, this is very much an understanding we should contest with the argument that quantitative research is value laden and socially produced. While recognizing that statistical data and techniques are valuable resources, we should also acknowledge their limitations and assert their failure to attain *neutral* and *objective* knowledge. Let us consider these issues by looking at some concrete examples of engagement with statistical data.

In Chapter 2, secondary evidence was defined as that produced sometime after the original event to which it refers, or by people not directly involved with the study in which it was originally generated. Building on this we can say that secondary statistical data are those analysed and organized for a purpose other than that intended by the researcher who originally collected them. For instance, surveys such as the National Census, the General Household Survey and the British Crime Survey are conducted by the government, to serve governmental purposes, and the categories used, and questions asked, are specific to purposes of governance. However, they also provide valuable sources of secondary data for sociologists. This can be illustrated by reference to Tables 3.1 and 3.2 in Chapter 3 of *Social Differences and Divisions*, reproduced here also as Tables 3.1 and 3.2.

Table 3.1   Employees[1]: by gender and occupation, United Kingdom, 1991 and 1999

| | Percentages | | | |
| | Males | | Females | |
Occupation	1991	1999	1991	1999
Managers and administrators	16	19	8	11
Professional	10	11	8	10
Associate professional and technical	8	9	10	11
Clerical and secretarial	8	8	29	26
Craft and related	21	17	4	2
Personal and protective services	7	8	14	17
Selling	6	6	12	12
Plant and machine operatives	15	15	5	4
Other occupations	8	8	10	8
All employees[2] (=100%) (millions)	11.8	12.4	10.1	10.8

Notes:
1 At Spring each year. Males aged 16 to 64, females aged 16 to 59.
2 Includes a few people who did not state their occupation. Percentages are based on totals which exclude this group.
Source of data: Labour Force Survey, Office for National Statistics.
Source: Office for National Statistics, 2000, Chart 4.13, p.72

Table 3.2   Population of working age[1]: by employment status and gender[1], United Kingdom, Spring 1999

| | Population in millions | | |
	Males	Females	All
Economically active			
In employment			
Full-time employees	11.4	6.2	17.7
Part-time employees	0.9	4.6	5.6
Self-employed	2.2	0.7	3.0
Others in employment[2]	0.1	0.1	0.2
All in employment	14.7	11.7	26.4
Unemployed[3]	1.1	0.6	1.7
All economically active	15.8	12.3	28.2
Economically inactive	3.0	4.8	7.8
Population of working age	18.8	17.1	35.9

Notes:

1 Males aged 16 to 64, females aged 16 to 59.

2 Those on government employment and training schemes and unpaid family workers.

3 Based on the International Labour Organization (ILO) definition.

Source of data: Labour Force Survey, Office for National Statistics.

Source: Office for National Statistics, 2000, Chart 4.2, p.66

As you can see, the data in these tables were compiled from official government statistics, originally collected for the purposes of government itself. However, Linda Janes, the author of Chapter 3 in *Social Differences and Divisions*, uses them as secondary data as part of an activity on the interpretation of changes in jobs and occupations by gender in the UK in the 1990s. What issues does this raise? To answer this, we need to remind ourselves what Janes does with the statistics. She writes:

> So women are primary workers in the new economy, but what sorts of jobs do they do? Table 3.1 demonstrates some clear divisions between men's and women's jobs, and some indications of gradual change. Men predominate in manual and craft-related occupations as well as in managerial and administrative work. Although women's participation in these more prestigious jobs is increasing, men's is not decreasing. Women predominate in selling and personal service work, as well as in secretarial and clerical occupations, although they do less of this work now than ten years ago. Table 3.1 does not delineate different levels within these occupational categories, but we know from other sources how few women there are in the most senior management and professional positions. The glass ceiling and the glass wall are popular metaphors that describe the difficulties women have in securing 'top' jobs in mixed professions or jobs at all in those associated solely with men ... .

> **(Janes, 2002, p.109)**

The first part of this quotation is devoted to extracting information from the tables. Janes then puts forward possible explanations for the figures. These official statistics have provided her with a useful set of data which would have been virtually impossible for an individual researcher to compile, given the amount of work and high costs involved. Janes works within the parameters which have been laid down by particular government departments. Of course, this suits the purposes of this particular piece of writing, but that might not have been the case if she had been interested in exploring different

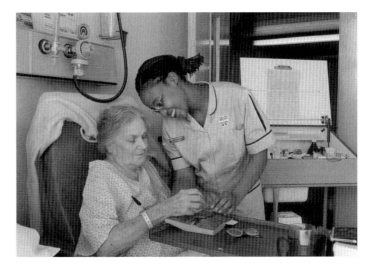

Figure 3.2 *Personal service jobs are often still seen as 'women's work'*

questions. Take, for example, the issue of women being in employment between the ages of 60 and 65 (as many women are) in order to build up retirement pension rights. Would the pattern in Table 3.1 have been different if these figures had been included, or if Janes had wanted to consider both men and women who continue to work beyond retirement age – as do, for example, members of parliament, medical consultants and self-employed people? Similarly, would the pattern have been different if Janes had been interested either in the question of whether the distribution of full-time and part-time work changes according to age, or in exploring the distribution of full-time and part-time workers between the different categories of work? She could not have got any of this information from Tables 3.1 or 3.2, nor from other *currently* published government statistics. This is because these other research questions are not, nowadays, part of the purpose of government information gathering. This can pose difficulties for sociologists who are interested in more specific research questions on a wider range of topics than are generally answerable from government statistics. Nevertheless, official statistics are a useful starting-point for social analysis and are often used as a source of secondary analysis, or as an informative background for further primary research.

As data do not speak for themselves, and are not simply 'technical' material, a responsible use of secondary data requires us to be clear about the nature of the data with which we are working. In his influential book *How to Lie with Statistics*, Huff (1973) suggests that a number of questions should be asked in order to assess numerical evidence. These are broadly referred to as considerations about the 'Who? When? What? Where? Why? and How?' of evidence.

1 *Who says?* Who is the author, or what is the origin of the information? Is there a vested interest? For example, government figures on the state of the National Health Service could be at considerable variance with figures produced by some health service trade unions. Also, we could be deceived by references to names of authority, and we should be aware of the kind of authority that is being lent to particular information.

2   *When was the information produced?* This is a vital question. If you look in *Social Trends* (an annual government publication containing a range of statistics on various aspects of society), you will find that, even in the most recent edition, figures are often at least two years old. Data in published academic texts are likely to be at least as old as this, because of the length of time between writing and publication. Take, for instance, the geodemographic information in Table 1.1 in Chapter 1 of *Social Differences and Divisions* **(Braham and Jones, 2002)**, which was taken from *The ACORN User Guide Index* (CACI, 2000). (As explained there, ACORN stands for **A C**lassification **o**f **R**esidential **N**eighbourhoods.) In order to have been published during 2000, the data will have been collected at least a year earlier – a concrete illustration of the considerable time lag there can be between production and publication. In order to assess when material was produced, it is also useful to know whether it is a 'snapshot' picture of a particular social situation (in which case it may be argued that it can apply only to a particular group at a particular time), or whether it shows trends over a period of time.

3   *What was the base for calculating the statistics? Has the base been changed?* This links to the previous point in that definitions, or the basis on which the statistics have been calculated, may change over time. For example, the basis on which unemployment figures have been calculated was changed 29 times during the 1980s. Thus, the challenge of carrying out a realistic comparison of unemployment rates over this period becomes considerable. See also **Murji's (2002)** discussion of racial categorisation in Chapter 4 of *Social Differences and Divisions*.

4   *Where is the population drawn from? Is there anything missing?* Quite often, you will not be told the actual number of people in the sample surveyed. In Table 3.1 above, what is the reader being told, or, perhaps more importantly, what is the reader *not* being told? The table gives the percentages of employees, by occupation and gender, in the UK workforce in 1991 and 1999. However, percentages refer to proportions, without any formal reference to the actual numbers of workers in each category. To get the numerical distribution, we have to work it out by using the figures at the bottom of the table, which tell us the number of employees in millions. This table provides the actual total figures, but many such tables are presented without this information, and if the source of the information is not given, then the reader cannot check accuracy or obtain other details. Actual total figures are not always necessary, however, if the aim is to examine relative proportions only.

5   *Why were the data collected in this way?* National data are collected by governments in a variety of ways, but the methods used are rarely stated when the statistics are published. The researcher wanting to question the data will have to search further for this information.

6   *How was the information obtained?* Statistical data used in research may come from both primary and secondary sources. Regardless of the source, there is a range of questions which the critical reader needs to ask: What

methods were used? How many respondents were there? How were decisions made on the categorization of the data? If this sort of information is not available when the data are presented, as is often the case, is the reader directed to where they may find it, should they need to go to the original source?

As Huff's points suggest, statistical data are by no means infallible, and a healthily sceptical view of both our own and others' facts and figures is required to ensure that any conclusions drawn from them can be justified. However, this certainly does not make statistics and other numerical data meaningless. Statistical data and techniques are valuable resources. The point is that it is necessary to scrutinize the social context in which they have been developed rather than simply accept or reject them outright. This scrutinizing is even more important when using secondary data, particularly in view of the many advantages of using this sort of quantitative material.

ACTIVITY I

Before reading further, list some of the advantages of secondary statistical data, based on your reading so far.

Some of the advantages of secondary statistical data you might have thought of include:

- Data have already been produced, often by organizations such as government and other official units, and they are generally available, which saves a great deal of time and money.
- They show patterns and trends over time, so comparisons can be made.
- Statistical information is often demanded as 'hard evidence' when putting forward particular arguments – as, for example, in relation to wealth, gender and 'race' inequalities – and is often influential in social policy decision making.

ACTIVITY 2

Have a look at a couple of newspapers or magazines and try to find reports which contain numerical data. You might make a comparison between a broadsheet and a tabloid newspaper, for example. Try to answer the six questions outlined above:

1 Who says?

2 When was the information produced?

3 What was the base for calculating the statistics? Has the base been changed?

4 Where is the population drawn from? Is there anything missing?

5 Why were the data collected in this way?

6 How was the information obtained?

SUMMARY OF SECTION 2

1　Quantitative research is socially produced, and quantitative data refer to information produced, analysed and presented in numerical form, usually as statistics.

2　Secondary quantitative data are produced by someone other than the researcher who makes use of them, and are often generated for a different purpose.

3　Secondary data are a useful source of information for social scientists, and may be the only source of information available.

4　Secondary statistical data derived from large data sets are both difficult to generate and very costly.

5　Secondary material must be read and used with care and it is useful to ask a number of basic questions about the process by which it was generated.

3　Quantitative research as social knowledge (2): producing primary data

When researchers are able to produce their own data, either by means of an individual research project or as part of a team of researchers in an organization, the data will be generated and organized in the way most suitable for their specific purposes. As suggested in Chapter 2, data of this type are generally referred to as 'primary data' and they will usually, though not exclusively, be the result of asking specific questions.

Asking and being asked questions are common experiences. Contemporary life habits and tastes have been closely scrutinized by market research, for instance, and people are often asked about preferences and experiences with regard to consumer products, political opinions, and so on. Surveys covering a vast range of topics are undertaken by commercial organizations, market research companies and government departments, and results are presented in the media on a regular basis. These data are generated according to particular requirements. One of the most commonly generated types of quantitative material in sociology and the social sciences more generally is the social **survey**.

survey

Social surveys are not new. For instance, surveys on poverty were conducted by Charles Booth in London and Seebohm Rowntree in York at the turn of the nineteenth and twentieth centuries. This was the first time that the extent of poverty in the UK had been researched and recorded in a detailed way and the surveys had far-reaching and ongoing effects on both the definition of and policy responses to it.

Survey research, as defined in the *Penguin Dictionary of Sociology*, 'is the systematic gathering of information about individuals and collectivities, using INTERVIEW or mail QUESTIONNAIRE methods to elicit information directly and interpreting the resulting data by means of statistical analysis' (Abercrombie *et al.*, 2000, p.352). The methods will vary according to the information being sought and the target population of the research, but, in general, they are based

Charles Booth 1902.

Figure 3.3   *Charles Booth (left) and Seebohm Rowntree*

on two broad types of questionnaire: open and closed. The kind of data to be generated will determine to a large extent the sort of questionnaire to be used, but both kinds have advantages and disadvantages.

Most often quantitative surveys employ **closed-ended questions**, which are designed to limit the choices of the respondent. Closed-question surveys are generally designed – and the questions framed in such a way – that the response given is kept as simple as possible. One way in which responses can be made is by ticking a box (see Figure 3.4).

closed-ended questions

Are you: **Female?** ☐   **Male?** ☐   (please tick one box)

Figure 3.4

Another method of categorizing responses is to use a Likert scale. This is a scaling technique – used to measure attitudes or views – in which respondents are asked to indicate a score or to circle a score in a given range. Figure 3.5, which is an adaptation of a question from a feedback form from a day school on an Open University course, shows a simple example of a Likert scale (you came across another example in the Leeds Dependency Questionnaire in Chapter 1, illustrated in Figure 1.4).

Please score the following on a scale of 1–5 (score 1 [low] 5 [high])

a) Were the day's objectives   Clear   Relevant to your needs   Met

☐   ☐   ☐

Figure 3.5

The question in Figure 3.5 could, however, have looked like that given in Figure 3.6.

Please circle the relevant number (score 1 [low] 5 [high])

a) **Were the day's objectives**	Clear	Relevant to your needs	Met
	1	1	1
	2	2	2
	3	3	3
	4	4	4
	5	5	5

Figure 3.6

This kind of data collection is very limiting because the researcher determines the range of possible answers, leaving no room for the respondent to move beyond the given categories. There may be no need for respondents to move beyond these categories, of course, and closed questions do allow for quick and easy enumeration and analysis of responses. However, while this technique may be useful in some ways, it is important to bear in mind that many measurement procedures pre-structure responses to particular questions, as discussed in Chapter 1, section 6.

Large-scale surveys are generally highly structured in this way and the questions are asked either by use of self-completed questionnaires (often postal), or by interviewing (by telephone or face-to-face), using a structured interview

Figure 3.7 *Dr David Wright administers a questionnaire as part of the 'Cultural Capital and Social Exclusion Project' based in the Sociology Department at The Open University, in collaboration with Manchester University*

schedule (a questionnaire used in interviewing), so that all the questions are asked of the target population in a standardized form and order. (Surveys are also beginning to be conducted via the internet.) Whichever method is used, the researcher should ensure that the data can be sorted and quantified easily.

Open-ended questions are designed to elicit more detailed information   **Open-ended**
from the respondent. Often, questionnaires include a 'sweep-up' question at   **questions**
the end – along the lines of, for example, 'Is there anything else you would like
to tell us?' or 'Any further comments would be very welcome'. A wealth of
information can be gleaned from this type of open-ended question which frees
the respondent from predetermined categories and moves more towards the
qualitative approaches of data generation, which were the subject of Chapter 2.

As stated earlier, it is our aim to examine the issue of quantitative research
as social knowledge not only in relation to the scrutiny of other researchers'
activities, but also in order to learn about and reflect on our own undertakings
in producing knowledge. With this is mind, we are going to explore next how
we might approach a simple piece of quantitative research using a questionnaire
with closed questions.

3.1   An exercise in primary data production

Imagine that you want to investigate why Open University students studying
DD201 in your region do or do not go to tutorials. You think that personal
circumstances such as having dependent children at home; distance from where
the tutorial is to take place; and the age of the student may have a bearing on
attendance. This is your basic hypothesis. As defined by *The Penguin Dictionary
of Sociology*, a **hypothesis** is a 'proposition or set of propositions put forward   **hypothesis**
for empirical testing. The word is often used more loosely to mean suggestion,
explanation or theory' (Abercrombie *et al.*, 2000, p.168). So, how do you go
about testing your hypothesis?

First of all, you are interested in whether or not students attend tutorials.
You could construct a fairly straightforward questionnaire with two basic
questions, as shown in Figure 3.8.

Are you a DD201 student in Region X? (Please tick one box)   **Yes** ☐   **No** ☐

Do you attend tutorials? (Please tick one box)   **Yes** ☐   **No** ☐

Figure 3.8

Can you see anything wrong with this questionnaire? What if someone is taking
two courses and cannot attend DD201 tutorials because they clash with tutorials
for the other course, which the student does attend? You might end up with a
'yes' answer in both boxes, and assume a link which may not be there, so you
would need to be specific and ask, 'Do you attend DD201 tutorials?' This may
sound straightforward, but it is easy to make this type of simple mistake, because
you know exactly what you mean by your question, but the respondent may
not.

Now, think about what further information you would want beyond that provided by these two questions. Remember that it is part of your reasoning that attendance at tutorials is linked to age, or perhaps distance from home, or whether the student has dependent children. Your questions might look something like those in Figure 3.9.

Are you a DD201 student in Region X? (Please tick one box)   **Yes** ☐   **No** ☐

Do you attend DD201 tutorials? (Please tick one box)   **Yes** ☐   **No** ☐

How old are you? ....

How far do you have to travel from home to the tutorial? ....

Do you have dependent children?   **Yes** ☐   **No** ☐

Figure 3.9

ACTIVITY 3

So, what have you now? Look at your questions, and at the last three in particular. Do you notice anything problematic about them?

We came up with the following:

1   There is a mixture of questions – there are both *open* and *closed* questions: some with 'yes'/'no' answers and some requiring factual information, which may confuse respondents.

2   Looking at the last three questions, particular concerns can be raised. Questions of a personal nature such as income, sexual behaviour or age, are regarded as 'stop' questions, because they often stop the respondent from answering further questions. In our questionnaire, age is central to the research, so how do we get round the problem? A number of techniques have been used:

(a) The most common method for collecting data on age is to categorize. For example, rather than asking someone's age directly, a range of ages may be given – say, 18–20; 21–30; 31–40; 41–50, and so on. Income can similarly be categorized.

(b) Potential 'stop' questions should be left to the end. That way, even if respondents do not answer a particular 'stop' question, they may perhaps still return the questionnaire with the other questions completed, and if you are interviewing, you will at least have most of the data you require.

3   The question concerning 'how far' students have to travel seems to be fairly straightforward, but in fact it is not. For instance, some students might interpret the question to mean 'how long does your journey take?' and give an answer in terms of hours or minutes, while others might interpret it in

terms of distance travelled. You could thus end up with a wide range of different responses, which would then have to be grouped. Here again, it would be logical, and time-saving, to group when the question is set. So, for example, you could specify that you require the information to be given in miles. But what if you have to travel two and a half miles to the tutorial? Because it is difficult to divide distance and time, it is necessary to allow for this, so we would have categories of 1 mile or less; between 1 and 3 miles; between 4 and 6 miles; and more than 6 miles. You would also need to be clear, of course, about what you meant by distance – is that one way, or there and back? Another problem to consider is that students may travel to tutorials straight from work, and you may wish to build this in as another question. An additional problem is that time taken to do the journey may be more important than distance. Perhaps you should ask about both distance and time, although in our example here we will restrict the information to distance.

4   So what of the final question? We have also forgotten to include instructions for this, and while it may at first seem obvious what we want to happen here, on closer examination we can see that it might not be very clear after all. Clarity of instruction is vital when a self-completed questionnaire is used, so that respondents know exactly what to do. It should be clear whether they have to circle, tick, number, or grade, and so on. Where you have a mixture of required responses, it is a good idea to group together questions of a similar type and to give one instruction rather than repeating instructions. Ambiguity often arises when we assume that the respondent knows what we are asking about. 'Do you have dependent children?' for example, could elicit a 'yes' response. But 'yes' to what? In what way are the children dependent? Parents may respond with a 'yes' if their child is a 19-year-old who is at university and dependent upon them for income; others may say 'no' if their child is a 14-year-old whom they consider able to feed, wash and generally look after themselves without too much supervision. We may decide that age is important and whether or not the children live at home. We might also want to know how many children there are.

By now, you will have a much longer questionnaire for your quite simple hypothesis. Of course, you may also wish to know about the *frequency* with which people attend tutorials, not just whether they attend, so you would need to incorporate this too. You might pose the question, 'How often do you attend tutorials?' If you are looking for an easily quantifiable answer, then you might offer: 'sometimes', 'regularly', 'not very often', and so on. But these words mean different things to different people. 'Regularly' can mean every week, every month or every year. For example, many women go for breast health screening regularly – every three years! There is a need to be specific and to avoid ambiguities and misunderstandings. If it is important to your research to know how many times someone attends tutorials, then pin the question down so that you get a clear and unambiguous response to a clear and unambiguous question. You would also want to number the questions for ease of **coding** and analysis,   **coding** so the questionnaire would now look like that shown in Figure 3.10.

1 Are you a DD201 student in Region X? (Please tick one box)   **Yes** ☐   **No** ☐

2 How many DD201 tutorials have you attended this year? (Please tick one box)   **None** ☐

1–4 ☐

5–8 ☐

9 or more ☐

3 Do you have children living at home? (Please tick one box)   **Yes** ☐   **No** ☐
   If 'Yes', please indicate the number in each age group:

Aged under 5 ☐

5 and under 10 ☐

10 and under 16 ☐

16 and over ☐

4 How far do you have to travel from home to the tutorial and back?   **Less than 1 mile** ☐
   (Please count a return journey and tick one box)

1–3 miles ☐

3–6 miles ☐

more than 6 miles ☐

5 What is your age range? (Please tick one box)   **18–20** ☐

21–30 ☐

31–40 ☐

41–50 ☐

51–60 ☐

60+ ☐

Figure 3.10   We could go on adding in different variables, but the intention here is to give
                   you a flavour of what has to be considered when constructing a questionnaire.
                   What you need to remember is that the more variables you add, the longer the
                   questionnaire and the more complicated the analysis. Our questionnaire is quite
                   short and straightforward, but questionnaires are frequently much longer and
                   more complicated than this. In these instances, it is necessary to consider other
                   factors in the production of the data.
                        Apart from the questions you choose to ask, their precision and their
                   relevance to the people being surveyed, the length of the questionnaire also
                   matters, as a long questionnaire may not be answered at all, especially by busy
                   people. The logical sequence of questions also needs to be considered. People

can deal much more easily with questions which are logically ordered, rather than those which jump all over the place. As we mention in points 3 and 4 in the list above, grouping questions together makes the topics clearer to the respondent; it also makes analysis of the data easier.

Language also needs to be clear and direct, and to be appropriate for the sample being researched. It is very easy to use jargon which others may not understand, and any possible ambiguity should be avoided. It can be difficult to find the balance between presupposing a particular level of educational achievement and appearing to be patronizing, but it is important to strive to do so. Leading questions should also be avoided. Memory is always a problem – drawing on memory has the potential to affect data, and you should be aware of this when data you are examining result from a question that depended on memory for a response.

3.2   Further issues raised by questionnaires

Even if you have no intention of doing research yourself, only of reading other people's, you still need to be aware of the issues involved in creating a survey. To some extent, when reading the results of other people's research, you have to take on trust that issues such as those we have discussed above have been considered, but if you have access to the actual questionnaire, you can check some of the detail for yourself. Inaccuracies in questionnaires raise the crucial question of the **validity** of the data. Validity concerns the degree to which the results of a study are true to the situation investigated, and this can be greatly increased if researchers conduct a **pilot study** before embarking on the main data collection. A pilot study is a 'dummy run' of the data collection. In a pilot study it is sufficient to carry out interviews with the standard questionnaire on a small group of individuals who could reflect the difficult cases that are expected to be encountered in the actual investigation. This exercise would enable you to reassess and amend the questionnaire as necessary.

validity

pilot study

The validity of data may also be compromised by *non-response* – either to the whole questionnaire, or to particular questions. Non-response is a serious problem with self-completed questionnaires. It may be that people who have not responded to the questionnaire comprise a particular group who differ in many ways from those who have responded; this might be a group which would provide more interesting and relevant data for the research. If you are not doing research yourself, you should also be aware that, as a critical reader, the response rate is important, and if this information is given, it enables you to assess the validity of the data.

As we mentioned earlier, questionnaires can be applied by post, completed by telephone, carried out face-to-face, or (though still relatively rarely) done via the internet. *Structured face-to-face interviewing*, using an interview schedule, has a wide range of applications in data collection, from reputable social research to market research on virtually anything. A schedule completed by an interviewer in face-to-face interviewing allows for more control over the interview situation in that the interviewer asks the questions and is able to prompt or clarify anything the respondent does not understand. A trained and experienced interviewer is much more able to handle a complex questionnaire and reduce the possibility of response errors. However, *response errors* cover a range of issues and can include those responses which respondents think will show them in a positive or negative light in the eye of the researcher. This raises a dilemma. On the one hand, the situation needs to be as natural as possible. On the other hand, it is important that the interviewer responds to questions and prompts the respondent to ensure understanding. How might an interviewer approach this? In a large-scale enquiry with more than one interviewer, it is essential that extensive training is provided, and for there to be collaboration and co-operation between the interviewers in order to ensure a unified approach. Even so, researchers cannot hope to present themselves in exactly the same way or expect the same interaction with all the people they interview – each of us reacts in different ways with different people.

ACTIVITY 4

Although our 'tutorial attendance' questionnaire has been prepared to be completed by the respondent, imagine that you are going to interview other DD201 students for the tutorial attendance investigation using the questionnaire in a structured interview. Can you think of any ways in which you could get round the problem of what is generally termed 'interviewer bias' (in which preconceived assumptions are imposed upon the situation)?

You might perhaps have thought of the following points:

- A similar approach is necessary towards everyone to be interviewed.
- Your approach should be non-directive and non-judgemental.
- The introduction to the topic will need to be considered, as will the questions and the way in which they are to be asked, so that your respondents are not led into giving an 'appropriate' answer rather than saying what they really think.
- You will perhaps want to follow Robson's (1993) advice for interviewers carrying out structured interviews:

    (a) Dress in a similar way to those you will be interviewing. If in doubt, err on the side of neatness and neutrality.

    (b) Be pleasant. Try to make the respondent comfortable.

    (c) View yourself as an actor, with the interview schedule as your script. Know it thoroughly.

    (d) Use the exact wording of questions and keep to their sequence.

    (e) Record the answers exactly. Don't make cosmetic adjustments, correct or fabricate words or arguments.

    (f) Use the standard probes only (a period of silence; an enquiring glance; 'mmhmm'; repeating back all or part of what the interviewee has just said).

3.3   The production of samples

sampling

Sampling is about selecting whom we should interview, what and how many documents to collect, or which settings to observe, and is a concept linked to the general laws of probability and statistics. As we mentioned in Chapter 2, samples are also inextricably bound up with the theoretical aspects of the research.

In quantitative research, sampling methods affect two main issues: the representativeness of the sample and the generalizability of the research findings. Representativeness refers to how accurately the sample reflects the characteristics of the broader population. This applies whether the population to be sampled consists of that of the United Kingdom, or all the Indian restaurants in Yorkshire. Generalizability refers to the degree to which the findings from one setting are likely to apply to similar settings. To select a sample, researchers normally use pre-existing lists (for example, a telephone directory or electoral register), which

Figure 3.11 *The size of the population involved often means that it is necessary to survey a representative proportion or 'sample' of it*

are called sampling frames. If these are inadequate, both the representativeness of the sample and the generalizability of the research findings will not be correct. Rigorous sampling strategies provide a firm basis for the investigation and enhance the strength of the claims that can be made about the material collected. Researchers use sampling techniques to explore the relationship of particular issues between the sample and a wider population. When sampling, representativeness is constructed in terms of the known characteristics of the people selected or units specified for sampling (for example, their distribution according to age or ethnicity).

Researchers can choose to interview, or send questionnaires, to the *whole population* (also referred to as the target population) to which their investigation applies, or to a proportion, or a *sample* of it (the survey population). Choice may well be determined by the number in the particular target population. A sample might be:

■ Random: where representativeness is sought by means of randomized selection. People sometimes assume that randomized selection means nothing more than 'at the whim of the researcher'. In fact, to guarantee the representativeness of the sample, randomized selection aims to ensure an equal, or known, chance of everyone in the target population being interviewed (for example, an individual in the target population might have a one in eight or other known chance of being interviewed with all and only these individuals being surveyed and all non-responses recorded).

■ Cross-sectional: in this a sample will be representative of all the different sub-groups in the target population. Random criteria can be applied within cross-sectional sampling selection.

■ Specific: where the sample is confined to one area, either geographically or socially. The entirety of this small group may then be included, or selection procedures by means of randomized or cross-sectional criteria may be applied.

SUMMARY OF SECTION 3

1   Primary data collection is that which is done for the researcher's own purpose, whether the researcher is an individual or an organization. The data are collected and organized in the way most suitable for the researcher's purposes.

2   A common method of collecting primary numerical data is the social survey. This can be large scale and highly structured, covering a very large population such as the census; or smaller scale, such as a survey of student attendance at tutorials in a particular region.

3   The normal method for collecting primary data is by post, by telephone or face-to-face, using a structured questionnaire which can be self-administered, or administered by an interviewer. Surveys are also sometimes, though not frequently, administered via the internet. Whatever method is used, non-response may well bias the data.

4   A pilot study is a 'dummy run' of the data collection and should be conducted whenever possible to reveal potential problems. Failure to do this may introduce bias.

5   Having decided on the topic, the method(s) and the general (target) population, the researcher then has to decide on the sample size. Samples comprise the individuals selected from the target population, and to be included in the survey; or the settings to be observed; or the material to be collected. Knowing the type of sample and its representativeness is important in evaluating any analysis of the data.

---

4   Quantitative research as social knowledge (3): analysing and presenting the data

As previously suggested, facts do not speak for themselves – we need to organize them in order to interpret them. The aim is to transform data into information which can be used in this way. Using the case of our DD201 tutorial investigation, suppose that the questionnaires have gone out to students, and responses are being returned. How do you organize the data? This question would, of course, have been broadly addressed at the time of constructing your questionnaire, particularly in terms of the overall groupings and headings. But more specific analytic questions need to be asked now. The traditional model is to wait until all the data are in, although it is highly advisable to read the completed questionnaires as they are returned. This gives a 'feel' for the responses, particularly where both closed and open questions have been included. The early, tentative, analysis begins here and, usually, issues and patterns which had not been thought of will emerge.

This section will discuss the collation, initial analysis and methods of presenting the data collected using closed questions. Less structured data and 'open' questions are discussed briefly at the end of the section, but essentially, their organization and analysis is very much the same as that discussed in relation to qualitative methods in Chapter 2.

With highly structured data, such as those in the census, or some of the government tables we have been discussing, the categories are predetermined, and computerized statistical packages are used. There are many statistical packages available to the social scientist (such as SPSS – the Statistical Package for Social Scientists; Minitab; and Statview).

If there is only a small amount of data, or a short questionnaire like our student questionnaire, or the preference is not to use the computer, the data can be collated and analysed manually, though this can be time-consuming. How do we start to organize the data in the case of our tutorial attendance investigation? The easiest way is to have a blank of your original questionnaire as a 'master' and to mark it with one tick or line for each response to each section. Having worked through all the questionnaires, a composite of all the responses will be produced. You can then add up all your little marks. Let us assume that the responses are as shown in Figure 3.12.

Figure 3.12

1 Are you a DD201 student in Region X? (Please tick one box)   **Yes** 29   **No** 0

2 How many DD201 tutorials have you attended this year? (Please tick one box)   **None** 7

1–4 5

5–8 11

9 or more 6

3 Do you have children living at home? (Please tick one box)   **Yes** 20   **No** 9
  Please indicate the number in each age group:

Aged under 5 3

5 and under 10 6

10 and under 16 8

16 and over 3

4 How far do you have to travel from home to the tutorial and back?   **less than 1 mile** 1
  (Please count a return journey and tick one box)

1–3 miles 4

3–6 miles 11

more than 6 miles 13

5 What is your age range? (Please tick one box)   **18–20** 1

21–30 5

31–40 10

41–50 8

51–60 4

60+ 1

Here, we have begun the first of two different levels of analysis: descriptive and exploratory/explanatory.

Descriptive analysis refers to when researchers say 'this is what I've got' – but it may not be what they thought they would get, which is why it is important not to have too fixed an idea of what is likely to emerge from the data. Openness of thinking is important, since it enables researchers to see what is there rather than what they think is there.

<hr>

ACTIVITY 5

What can we see in our data? Have a look at Figure 3.12 again and make a note of your answers. (For the purposes of the exercise you should assume there are 35 students in the region.)

Perhaps you noted the following:

- Question 1: there were 29 'yes's', and none in the 'no' category. The total number of students studying DD201 in your region was 35. Where are the remaining six? There are two possible answers here – either you missed some, or, if you have counted your questionnaires and have 29, then the missing ones are due to non-response.

- Question 2: the largest number of students attended tutorials quite regularly, but the second highest number did not attend at all.

- Question 3: about two-thirds of students have children living at home. Of these, the majority are aged over 5 and under 16.

- Question 4: the largest number of students have to travel more than 6 miles to tutorials, and very few live within a short distance of the study centre.

- Question 5: more than half of the students are aged between 31 and 50; the rest are divided almost equally between younger and older age ranges.

What about the original research hypothesis – that attendance at tutorials may be linked with age, or distance from home, or whether the student has dependent children? To draw this sort of information from the data we need to move on to exploratory and explanatory analysis.

Exploratory and explanatory analysis moves on from description to explore relationships within the data and relate these back to original ideas. Researchers need to accept at this stage that preconceived ideas or favourite theories may be brought into question. In the case of our tutorial attendance investigation, we have developed a hypothesis and we are collecting data to see whether our hypothesis can be supported. So now we need to see whether we can make any links within the data and whether any patterns are emerging. We are beginning to *explore* the data. The different levels of analysis – descriptive and exploratory/explanatory – are interrelated, since it is often only when the data from quantitative methods are collated and presented that patterns, trends and links can be more clearly seen and explored.

Have another look at your 'master' sheet. Can you make any links or see any patterns? It is impossible to see from this whether tutorial attendance is affected by age, distance or children. This means that you need to go back to the original questionnaires and sort the data in different ways. You have probably realized that the data can be sorted by attendance, number of children, distance and age. But how would you go about this? As there are only 29 questionnaires, this is not too difficult a task to do by hand, though as we mentioned above, it can be somewhat time-consuming.

Let us start with age. You need to separate out the six categories of age on to six separate 'master' sheets. Then sort through your questionnaire responses and note them down on to those six sheets and see whether patterns are emerging – it is likely, though not inevitable, that they will be, but you will not be able to say with certainty which of the other criteria are most influential. To do this, you will need to take each of the other criteria and do a similar exercise. This *is* time-consuming to do manually, even with a small number. You can imagine that the task would be virtually impossible with larger numbers and this is where you would reap the benefit of one of the computer packages designed to do just this sort of job.

By this stage, you may well have realized that it would probably have been helpful to have asked, 'Which (if any) of these factors were the main influence on tutorial attendance?' Of course, there could be other factors which prevent people attending tutorials – particularly for the seven students who have never attended, and a further question could have been added to address this. These two questions, along with an opportunity at the end for students to add 'any other comments', would then have made analysis much easier, and would have added a qualitative aspect to the data.

As discussed in Chapter 1, sociological concepts need to be rendered into a form susceptible to measurement for them to be treated like an object. The example given in Chapter 1 of such a concept was alcohol dependence. In the imagined project we have outlined here it is tutorial attendance. We have operationalized the concept in order to measure it by identifying key variables related to it, and from that we begin to question the relationships between variables.

When analysing research material the key concern is with establishing relationships between events, situations or variables. In quantitative studies these relationships are usually drawn on a statistical basis in relation to specific variables. As Chapter 1 explained, these relationships are referred to as correlations and they can be negative or positive, depending upon how different variables relate to one another – although remember that relationships are not necessarily causal (you may want to remind yourself of these points by looking back to Chapter 1, section 5.3). You should note as well that the '**significance**' **significance** of any apparent relationship also has to be established, meaning that, via statistical analysis, the researcher must discount the possibility that the relationship has occurred by random chance.

Correlation comes into some of the questions used in our survey of tutorial attendance above. Take, for example, the question about how having dependent children at home may affect students' attendance at tutorials. The basis of analysis by which this would need to be answered would involve 'crossing' the variable of tutorial attendance with the variable relating to dependent children at home. Having done this, it may be found that a correlation exists by which those caring for dependent children are found to attend fewer tutorials than those with no children at home, or vice versa.

The next stage is how to present the information collected. The presentation of data is most often part of the analytical process, as we indicated in Chapter 2, yet one that comes at the end of that process, when the researcher publishes their results or gives a talk about their research. Data can therefore be presented in narrative form, or diagrammatically (by use of graphs or other visual methods), and they can be presented verbally. With a computer package, this stage of the analysis is relatively easy and numerical data can be presented in a variety of ways. We come across some of these every day, in newspapers, magazines, reports and advertising. They include written reports, tables, graphs, bar and pie charts, and so on. Data can also be presented using a combination of such methods and techniques, and it is important to take this into consideration.

As we noted in Chapter 2, quantitative and qualitative methods may be combined, and as we mentioned in section 3 above, some questionnaires designed to construct numerical data, may also include some open-ended questions. These produce qualitative data, which may be difficult to quantify to enable numerical representation. They are relatively easy to manage if there are just a few questionnaires, but a large sample, or lengthy written responses, can be very time-consuming to deal with. In this case, the researcher will categorize the answers under broad headings. However, open-ended questions included in a structured questionnaire are designed to add a qualitative dimension to the research findings – the value of such qualitative data is that verbatim material adds richness to the text of the research report when used to illustrate points being made. However, qualitative data, when used in this way, give rise to many of the problems we discussed in Chapter 2, and require an analytical approach closer to that designed for qualitative research.

The important point to remember about categorizing data is that this involves an element of choice. Different categories will present a different picture, regardless of whether our data are qualitative or quantitative. Imagine for a moment that we changed the age groups in our tutorial attendance questionnaire. This would put different numbers of students into different categories and present a different picture. This element of choice in categorization applies not only to our data here, of course, but to all data, and you need to be aware of this as a researcher and critical reader.

SUMMARY OF SECTION 4

1   Analysis is necessary because facts do not speak for themselves.

2   Quantitative analysis is easier if its format is considered seriously by the researcher at the start of the research.

3   There are two types of analysis – descriptive and exploratory/explanatory. Descriptive analysis gives basic factual information, organized in a particular way. Exploratory/explanatory analysis moves on from this and explores relationships within the data, relating these back to original ideas.

4   In general, the choice of presentation of data will be influenced by the aims of the researcher. Some standard questions need to be asked when examining any data. The ways in which particular data are presented are also influenced by analytical concerns.

5   Sometimes data can give rise to apparently conflicting information, so it is important to examine the various forms of presentation carefully to ensure that the data presented are saying what you think they are saying.

5   Conclusion: epistemological and ethical assumptions of quantitative research

We stated at the beginning of this chapter that quantitative research methods are produced in social contexts which need to be examined for an appreciation of the particular kind of knowledge that research based on quantification creates. We mentioned that the practices of research traditionally associated with quantitative approaches have been criticized for their assumed neutrality and the treatment of evidence as factual and objective. Other criticisms include whether 'head counting' can express complex social reality, and the tendency of quantification to impose categories on meanings and to treat people as 'just numbers' (Tonkiss, 1998).

In this chapter we have contested the view of neutrality in quantitative approaches to research, and indicated many ways in which researchers need to scrutinize the context of the production of numerical data and their presentation. This practice is not dissimilar to that which we discussed in Chapter 2 in relation to qualitative research, although the instruments and techniques employed are different. For instance, it is very important to accept that the practice of measurement itself tends to alter what is measured. We noted when discussing Huff's (1973) *How to Lie with Statistics* that changes in the basis upon which statistics are calculated may change the statistics themselves (and thus potential relationships between variables). For instance, if we were to measure the whole of the student population of DD201 we might well get a different picture of tutorial attendance from the one we generated when investigating just one particular region. It is equally important to question whether statistical data present a static picture of a social world that is, in reality, always changing. Yet, quantitative data provided by the census or large social surveys produce useful knowledge about society, allowing examination of patterns and distributions and the interrogation of social processes.

Researchers have at their disposal the option to combine a range of methods within the quantitative and qualitative approaches (Bryman, 1988; Brannen, 1992). As we saw in Chapter 2, ethnographic participant observation methods may be combined with semi-structured interviews (both of which are qualitative approaches). Similarly, statistical data from census material can be used together with quantitative survey data within combined quantitative methods. The combination of research methods, however, brings differences to the fore, even when, as stressed in this chapter, both quantitative and qualitative approaches are interpreted as knowledge produced in particular social contexts. The integration of different methods therefore requires careful consideration, because it involves combining not only data acquired by different methods, but also the assumptions and practices of the data generation process. It is important that researchers are aware of the implications of combining methods and material.

It is widely acknowledged in the social sciences that epistemology plays a key role in methodological decisions because it constitutes the principles and rules by which a researcher decides whether and how social phenomena can be known, and how knowledge can be demonstrated. As discussed in the Introduction to this book, epistemology refers to what counts as knowledge, to how we know what we know. All theoretical and empirical approaches in sociology presuppose (explicitly or implicitly) some epistemological position or other (Marshall, 1998), though there are several competing conceptual frameworks and any choice will have different implications. Researchers must recognize that there is more than one epistemology and that individual epistemologies are neither all complementary nor equally consistent with their definition of social reality (that is, their ontological position). As noted in Chapter 2, any research analysis is considered valid when the methods and sources used enable one to elaborate the explanations and understandings one seeks.

To assume that quantitative methodology is objectively neutral implies an epistemological position different from the position asserting that quantification is produced in social contexts that need to be taken into account in the processes of the creation, evaluation and presentation of knowledge. This has a bearing on the issue of values, as discussed in Chapter 1. Researchers cannot avoid involvement and risk – the world to be known has an impact on the knower, and vice versa, and power is always present in research environments, even if in an abstract and hidden form. All of this needs to be taken into account, too, with regard to the epistemological position we have adopted in this chapter. This is why we have suggested that the handling of secondary data from census and government or marketing research agencies' surveys requires an examination of their historical perspectives, conceptual frameworks, intended use as social products and supposedly rational and disinterested production. Likewise, we have emphasized the need for the researcher to reflect on these dimensions when producing, analysing and presenting their own numerical data sets.

Researchers need to be aware of the strengths and weaknesses of quantitative research in order to deploy its methods in the optimum way. These strengths and weaknesses can be summarized as follows.

Strengths of quantitative research

1   Quantitative research belongs to a powerful and recognized research tradition which is perceived to be valid. It provides a sound basis for claiming that one knows something.

2   Quantification provides useful knowledge to permit the examination of the patterns and distribution of social processes, as well as their interrogation.

3   Quantitative approaches are especially efficient for exploring the large-scale, 'structural' features of social life.

4   Quantitative methods readily allow researchers to establish relationships among variables.

5   Quantitative methods enable researchers to make generalizing claims and sound arguments about the social world.

Weaknesses of quantitative research

1   Quantitative data are usually produced by someone other than the researcher and are often produced for purposes that are not always easy to assess.

2   Quantitative research is often expensive to undertake.

3   Quantitative approaches are usually driven by the concerns of funding agencies and the researchers, leaving no room for the expression of the concerns of research participants.

4   Quantitative methods risk imposing the researcher's values on those being researched and often fail to capture the participant's point of view.

5   Quantitative methods are weak in exploring the reasons for relationships between variables.

Part of the process of balancing the strengths and weaknesses of quantitative research rests on the ways in which ethics are approached. As stated in Chapter 2, ethical concerns need to play a prominent part in any research design. The production of an ethical research design is as important as the production of an intellectually coherent product. Ethics should be taken account of from the framing of research questions to the final presentation of data. Research ethics are a complex matter and there is no unique ethical solution to all research issues. Ethical, moral and political questions should be at the forefront of each step of the research process. This involves questioning purposes, interests and implications, which, though they may not immediately raise ethical issues, will identify complex problems the research may touch upon. Such issues include the researcher's own experience, ethical position, and professional culture; and the codes of practice of the professional body and legal frameworks concerned. As we noted in Chapter 2, ethical issues in research are applicable to both qualitative and quantitative approaches, and you should recall the concerns raised in that chapter when assessing knowledge produced by means of quantitative procedures.

The uses to which sociology has been put in the real world are closely connected with the epistemological, ontological and ethical issues discussed in relation to research methods in both Chapter 2 and this chapter. These uses are explored in the next chapter.

References

Abercrombie, N., Hill, S. and Turner, B.S. (2000) *The Penguin Dictionary of Sociology* (4th edn), Harmondsworth, Penguin.

Braham, P. and Janes, L. (eds) (2002) *Social Differences and Divisions*, **Oxford, Blackwell/The Open University.**

Brannen, J. (1992) *Mixing Methods: Qualitative and Quantitative Research*, Aldershot, Ashgate.

Bryman, A. (1988) *Quantity and Quality in Social Research*, London, Unwin Hyman.

CACI (2000) *The ACORN User Guide Index*, London, CACI Limited.

Huff, D. (1973) *How to Lie with Statistics*, Harmondsworth, Penguin.

Irvine, J., Miles, I. and Evans, J. (eds) (1979) *Demystifying Social Statistics*, London, Pluto Press.

Janes, L. (2002) 'Understanding gender divisions: feminist perspectives' in Braham, P. and Janes, L. (eds) *op. cit.*

Janes, L. and Mooney, G. (2002) 'Place, lifestyle and social divisions' in Braham, P. and Janes, L. (eds) *op. cit.*

Marshall, G. (1998) *Oxford Dictionary of Sociology*, Oxford, Oxford University Press.

Murji, K. (2002) 'Race, power and knowledge' in Braham, P. and Janes, L. (eds) *op. cit.*

Office for National Statistics (2000) *Social Trends 30*, London, Office for National Statistics.

Pocket Oxford Dictionary (2002) Oxford, Oxford University Press.

Robson, C. (1993) *Real World Research*, Oxford, Blackwell.

Savage, M. (2002) 'Social exclusion and class analysis' in Braham, P. and Janes, L. (eds) *op. cit.*

Tonkiss, F. (1998) 'The history of the social survey' in Seale, C. (ed.) *Researching Society and Culture*, London, Sage.

Purposes and practices of sociology

Peter Hamilton, Kenneth Thompson and Sophie Watson

Contents

1　Introduction

In this final chapter of *The Uses of Sociology*, we will be looking at the relationship of sociology to the world 'out there'. In other words, we will be asking the question, in what ways might sociology be useful? Sociology tries to make sense of the society in which – as we have seen throughout the course – it is by its nature deeply embedded. So, at the very least, sociology is an important subject to study, since it helps us make sense of the world. However, more ambitiously, it might be possible to argue that it provides us with the tools to change the world and to make it a better place in which to live. It is these and similar issues with which you will be engaging in the course of this chapter.

This chapter has three aims. First, in sections 1 and 2 it examines how sociologists have viewed the purposes of sociology, as an academic discipline, in competing ways. Three major perspectives are outlined, each of which has different implications for the practice of sociology in the real world. The second aim is then taken up in section 3, which considers various ways in which sociology as a set of ideas has been taken up outside the academy. The relationship of sociology and sociological knowledge to the world out there – sociology's engagement with the 'social' – involves a mutually constitutive or two-way process. That is, sociology simultaneously constructs the 'social' as well as being constructed by it. In other words, the practices of and ideas from sociology influence social action, which in turn provides food for thought and analysis for sociologists. This very real engagement of the academic discipline of sociology with the social world is one of the reasons why sociology is such an exciting area of intellectual enquiry.

Having considered the different perspectives on the purposes of sociology, and some of the uses to which it has been put, in section 4 the chapter reflects on some possible uses of sociology in the twenty-first century. In particular, we ask: how can sociology best renew its sense of purpose as it moves into the twenty-first century?

AIMS

The aims of this chapter are:

1　To examine some of the competing ways in which sociologists view the purposes of sociology:

- the 'rational-scientific' perspective
- the 'political' perspective
- the 'sociology as theory' perspective.

2　To explore some of the uses of sociology in the world 'out there'.

3　To consider some future uses for sociology in the twenty-first century.

2   Sociology and social action

From its origins in Enlightenment thought during the eighteenth century, the ways in which sociology relates to society and social action have been a key concern of the discipline. This section identifies some of the key themes of sociological debate about its uses – its 'practice' – and discusses the main intellectual threads through which the encounter between the intellectual activity of sociology and its wider social and political context has been maintained.

As we saw in Chapter 1, one way of mapping the key epistemological and ontological traditions in sociology is in terms of an opposition between competing positivist and interpretivist approaches. This discussion concerned what constituted authoritative knowledge in sociology. In the present chapter we see how these traditions have informed and underpinned sociologists' perspectives on the purposes of sociology in the real world, that is, the relationship of sociology to social action. We consider how implicit within the positivist and interpretivist traditions are particular ideas about the purposes of sociology. The three main approaches discussed are the 'rational–scientific, the 'political' and the 'sociology as theory' perspectives. You might like to refer back to the introduction to Chapter 1 where it was argued that Bourdin's view of sociology's utility, echoing Comte's, was as 'an instrument for organizing the present and imagining the future'. As you read further in the present chapter, you will see how this positivist tradition within sociology has influenced, and given rise to, the rational–scientific perspective on the purposes of sociology in the real world. You will see also how the 'sociology as theory' perspective derives some of its ideas from the interpretivist tradition, while the 'political' perspective borrows its ideas from both these traditions. While these connections are real, it is important to remember that the relationships between the perspectives discussed here, and the sociological traditions discussed in Chapter 1, are complex and not always easily mapped. However, what you will find is that sociological perspectives on the purposes of sociology in the real world have been influenced by, and bear the indelible traces of, these epistemological debates.

What is clear about the relationship between sociology and its practical role – its 'uses' – is that the key debates have concerned the nature of sociology itself, and have influenced its theories and subject matter from its emergence as a discipline in the eighteenth and nineteenth centuries to the present day. We might even say that sociology has been very much defined by what sociologists thought it could be used for. This is mainly because sociology has had to advocate its utility, rather than being a necessary instrumental form of knowledge or technique serving an established profession.

There are three general ways of approaching this issue:

- First, is sociology a way of knowing something more profound about human affairs?
- Second, is it an indispensable guide to socially transformative action?
- Third, is it a way of writing about society, of imagining what is distinctive about the social domain?

The argument advanced in this chapter is that these approaches have led to three very broad perspectives within sociology, each of which has been characterized by one of these approaches to (or modes of engagement with) the social. If we were to argue that sociology should be 'useful' in a particular fashion – perhaps on the basis that by knowing more about how society works we can invent a method of 'improving' social processes – then we would focus on the perspective that we term 'rational–scientific', though it might as easily be called utilitarian ('useful') or even 'positivist' in the sense that it has often drawn on the positivist approach outlined in Chapter 1. By extension, sociology might also be seen as useful to those wanting to change society for political reasons, who see it as the servant of particular notions as to how society 'ought' to be organized. The point is that those who share these perspectives – the rational–scientific and the political – believe that sociology might have such uses. This determines their approach to sociology and how they construct their careers.

Yet, either as students of sociology or as sociologists in academic life, we are not forced to take the view that sociology is an inherently practical or useful discipline. Perhaps sociology does not have direct applications at all, in much the same way as theoretical physics often does not have a direct application to the world. From such a perspective, sociology might be better thought of as an intellectual pursuit, a way of talking and thinking about a 'society'. Some contemporary sociologists certainly take this view. For example, Goffman, as we shall see later, represents a 'sociology as theory' strand within sociology. This is a mode that has become more obvious in the 'post-modern' world, where much greater attention to the symbolic – signs, metaphors, representations and so on – now characterizes sociological writing. Sociological work of this type can be seen as having many affinities to literature, to work in the media industries, and as a form of 'commentary' about social life. This is not to suggest it is uncritical or politically unaware, but rather that it considers the practice of the rational–scientific and political perspectives to have been surpassed, no longer appropriate to modern life.

2.1   The three perspectives

The present image of sociology to many in the non-academic world tends to emphasize the often 'radical' position taken by its practitioners in the recent past – a time when various forms of Marxism were dominant. This is due in part to the political critique developed by radical and left-wing sociologists in the 1960s and 1970s. However, it is important to bear in mind that sociology is not inherently wedded to one political tradition, nor is it an intellectual discipline that has been organizationally yoked to any particular profession outside the university world. Although sociology has relevance to many occupations, the broad range of its concerns – which cover the economic, cultural and political dimensions of society – do not lead directly to a particular occupation apart from that of sociologist, which is a role most associated with education, and to some extent with organizations designed to provide statistical information about the population to charities, state bodies or international agencies. Nevertheless, you will discover in section 4.1 that in the late 1990s and into the early 2000s sociology entered into a close relationship with government through its association with the agendas of the 'third way' as represented in the UK by New Labour.

Although the 'rational–scientific' perspective is distinct from the 'political' perspective, it should be clear that to be 'rational–scientific' is not to be apolitical in the sense of being wholly separate from politics. However, those working within this perspective tend to see sociology as an intellectual practice designed to elicit objective information about social processes and structures, and to make it available as information open to scrutiny and debate. Political values or policy matters may well be the source of the problems studied by those working in the rational-scientific mode. The information produced may also become part of the manifesto programme of a political party. Nevertheless, most crucially, those working in this mode would argue that intellectual and political interests should be seen as separate.

In contrast, 'political' perspectives stress the intimate interconnectedness of political values with sociological theory: traditions from Marxism to feminism (but also some conservative traditions) can be identified here. According to such approaches, sociological knowledge is inherently political because it deals with the organization of society. Only by testing this knowledge via intervention in the real world of social action can its validity be assessed. It must offer a theory of action or practice which contributes to the reorganization or emancipation of society.

Finally, there is a growing domain of cultural and theoretical sociology (especially but not exclusively contemporary work) which is relatively uninterested in political issues in the broader sense, though it may have moral and philosophical concerns. This perspective of 'sociology as theory' sees sociology's role as describing and making sense of society. To put this another way, this is the idea of 'sociology for its own sake'.

For instance, when the US sociologist Erving Goffman (1972), who was discussed in Chapter 3 of *Understanding Everyday Life* **(Hamilton, 2002)**, wrote about 'role-playing' behaviour and described what he called the 'tie-signs' that couples use to signal their relationships to each other in public, it soon becomes clear what he was not doing. He was not offering a way of scientifically plotting the dynamics of couple relationships. Nor was he interested in creating knowledge about these relationships so that they can be changed or 'improved' in some way according to a political theory – of whatever colour.

Instead, Goffman's research involved a close and detailed observation of what went on in public places. He then thought about its dynamics, and about the 'little theatre' in which it took place, the public stage. Yet Goffman's books and articles are not at first sight literary works – although he seems to have written about social behaviour because the rich variety of human behaviour interested him, in much the same way as it might intrigue a novelist. Close attention to social attitudes and values can help a novelist produce wonderful stories, and offer insight into ways of life that are historically or culturally distant from the reader. In *Talking Heads*, Alan Bennett's monologues written for television, for instance, similar insights about character, about the little dramas of everyday life, appear and seem every bit as telling in their analysis of social behaviour as the best sociology. Indeed, Goffman's work appeals to literary writers; Bennett is in fact a great fan of his work, and has written an interesting essay about Goffman's approach (Bennett, 1994). But this is not its only appeal: many sociologists have also been inspired by his work, and have taken its ideas into both rational–scientific and political perspectives. Its role has been to entertain, interest and inspire. Clearly, then, we can't place Goffman easily within the rational–scientific or political perspectives – even if his work seems to be an important part of the sociological 'canon'.

**Baudrillard,
Jean**

Although Goffman's work is distinctive and unique, we might also identify other sociological writers who work in a similar way. In the late nineteenth century, the German sociologist Georg Simmel produced much of his work in the form of aphoristic essays, offering small 'snapshots' of life to which he would bring some sociological insight. A far more recent example would be the French sociologist **Jean Baudrillard**, whose work is perhaps as far from the 'rational-scientific' as could be imagined – one of his books, *America*, takes the form of a highly impressionistic account of US culture, as epitomized by Las Vegas (Baudrillard, 1986). Indeed, Baudrillard's writing seems so 'literary' or personal that many of his erstwhile sociological colleagues (he taught sociology for many years at the University of Nanterre near Paris) now regard him as no longer contributing to the discipline. Yet Baudrillard is one of the most widely read authors on contemporary culture, and his work is taught in sociology courses across the world. Baudrillard and Goffman have made a significant impact through developing such a form of sociological writing. These sociologists tend to reject universalism (that is, the search for accounts that are universally 'true'), and their writing is often relativistic and allusive.

These three views on how sociology and sociological knowledge relate to the real world are strong modes to which individual sociologists are drawn. They are reflected in differing forms of research – both qualitative and quantitative – as well as in writing and intellectual dissemination. But most of these have taken place within some aspect or another of the 'public sector' – the world of the university, the education system, government and administration. To confine our consideration of the relationship of sociology to social action to the 'public sphere' considered in that way would, however, be misleading. Although there may be few jobs advertised which include 'sociology' in their title, there are nonetheless many ways in which sociology as a form of knowledge and a practice is evident in private sector activities. This is particularly clear in marketing and sales organizations using various forms of market research, for example in the field of commerce (as we shall see later). Sociology's impact on wider society now seems to be increasingly transacted through its incorporation in the design and management of commercial, capitalist organizations, a situation that many radical sociologists would have considered unacceptable in the 1970s. In addition, in the form of the neo-liberal third way, it may even become part of government itself, as an integral element of the management and control of a capitalist society.

SUMMARY OF SECTION 2

1   There are differing perspectives on the purposes of sociology in the real world.

2   The three main perspectives are: rational–scientific, political and 'sociology as theory'.

3   Sociologists coming from the rational–scientific perspective see the main use of sociology as the production of better, useful (or positive) knowledge.

4   Sociologists coming from the political perspective view the main use of sociology as a guide to social change.

5   Sociologists coming from the 'sociology as theory' perspective see the main use of sociology as a way of representing the meanings of the social dimension.

3 Sociology's engagement with the 'social'

We will now turn to look in greater detail at each of the three perspectives.

3.1 The rational–scientific perspective

The French sociologist Pierre Bourdieu acted the role of the engaged and politicized intellectual; his ideas have informed political debate in France and made a vital contribution to giving sociology a new and important role within contemporary French society. Yet at the same time, he was always committed to the idea that sociology is a social science. Conceiving of sociology as a science implies the objectification of social relations, practices and ideas, so that they can be rationally and consensually discussed and made available to anyone capable of understanding the terminology in use and the theoretical system in which they operate (Robbins, 2000, p.15). The sociologist, Bourdieu maintained, must objectify the 'primary experience' of the social in order to analyse it scientifically.

In that sense Bourdieu took over an important tradition in sociology from his predecessor Emile Durkheim, who had sought to establish sociology as a new science in the late nineteenth century by 'treating social facts as things'. For both Bourdieu and Durkheim, understanding that sociology is concerned with the political – or that its conclusions might have political consequences – does not mean that it cannot be practised via rational–scientific techniques, and produce objective knowledge. As such, you won't be surprised to hear that sociologists who are most clearly linked with the 'rational–scientific' perspective often stress the importance of thinking of sociology as fundamentally akin to the natural sciences in its mode of operating.

In common with positivists, whom you came across in Chapter 1, sociologists working within the rational-scientific perspective tend to argue that sociologists can both discover facts about society that can be quantified and tested, and keep facts and values separate. For example, for those attached to the rational–scientific perspective, sociologists might investigate and quantify the level of poverty in a given population according to pre-specified indicators, such as income levels, health and housing levels, or access to basic resources; they might also be able to point to the social consequences of poverty, such as high crime rates; but they should not as sociologists use those facts to advocate particular policy solutions (see the discussion of 'value neutrality' in Chapter 1, section 8.3)

There has been a long tradition of sociologists working within this approach. In the late nineteenth

Figure 4.1 *The London School of Economics (LSE), founded in 1895 by Beatrice and Sidney Webb*

and early twentieth century Sidney Webb (1859–1947) and Beatrice Webb (1858–1943), who were leaders of the Fabian Society and founders of the London School of Economics (Figure 4.1), together with Charles Booth (1840–1916), inaugurated a sociological tradition of social investigation into the lives and experiences of the London poor. This tradition continued throughout the twentieth century with Peter Townsend's famous study of *Poverty in the UK* (1979) owing much of its analysis to these early predecessors. If you take a look back at *Social Differences and Divisions* **(Braham and Janes, 2002)**, you will see the influences of this approach. For example, Chapter 7 on education, housing and social justice derives much of its argument from the analysis of sociological statistics, which map the patterns of inequality in education and housing according to class, gender and ethnicity.

3.2   The political perspective

One of the major problems involved in sociology is its (apparent) embeddedness in social issues of the day. This is a two-way street. Activists of any persuasion can (and do) use the social knowledge created by sociology. Similarly, a sociologist may decide to get involved in some form of political or other action, perhaps with the aim of both advancing political goals and at the same time studying the action itself. This in turn may lead to the production of new sociological knowledge and theory. Certain consequences might follow, which include a whole range of ethical questions about whether the activism itself can be made 'public' through research. (If knowledge is power, should the activist organization be opened to scrutiny? How will the sociological knowledge be used? Do the participants need to be consulted before reference is made to them?) These questions about the relationship between sociology and activism have profound implications for the practice of sociology.

Such concerns have been present within the discipline since the nineteenth century. Max Weber and, more recently, Jürgen Habermas have taken one view: sociology can offer certain 'practical hints about the feasibility of realising certain values, but it cannot tell us whether or not we are right to pursue those ideals whatever the cost' (Outhwaite, 1996, pp.98–9). In contrast, those who advocate the 'political perspective' will tend to argue that sociology and sociologists cannot avoid making value judgements in their work and using this work for practical and political purposes (see also Chapter 1, section 8.3). From this perspective, sociology's dissemination and use, as well as the reasons for its construction in the first place, are irretrievably founded in political processes. The role of sociology, then, becomes one of emancipation and change: social knowledge is politically charged or, as Michel Foucault put it, 'power is always present'. A variant of this position has recently been argued by Alexander:

> There is a relativity at the heart of the sociological enterprise, one that represents an irrefutable dimension of the human sciences more generally. The relativity comes about because sociology is a human science rather than a science of nature. Max Weber understood the implications of this fateful distinction, but Marx, Durkheim, and Parsons did not. Yet, this fundamental fact explains the very distinctiveness of our discipline and our science, whatever that term may actually mean. It explains why Marx, Durkheim, Weber, and Parsons are still living classics, and why, at the same time, none among them could ever succeed in shaping the past, present, or future of sociology in their own image.

Sociological practitioners can never be as certain of their knowledge as natural scientists, and even when they feel certain, they aim to use their knowledge not only for explaining the world but also for changing it, that is, for moral purposes.

(Alexander, 2001, p.xv)

Perhaps the most significant impetus to the political perspective has come from Karl Marx's idea of 'praxis', or the notion that the only way of knowing the world is via the 'dialectical' interplay of action in and upon it, through which we come to know the world as we change it.

Historically, the era when this idea about praxis infused sociological thinking most fully was the 1960s and 1970s. This was precisely the moment when mass university education was emerging in the industrialized West, and particularly in the United States, France and Germany as the baby-boom population of those born just after the Second World War began to enter higher education. Sociology was a popular newly expanding discipline which was rapidly established in universities and colleges, and which appeared to offer some insight into contemporary conditions, and to be in tune with the social aspirations of this large social group. The Vietnam War, feminism, the student revolutions of 1968, racism, civil rights, apartheid in South Africa, emergent environmentalism, gay liberation, and the Cold War all loomed large as contemporary social issues, about which the new discipline might be expected to contribute some insights and also to offer solutions. Thus, we see the mutually constitutive relation of sociology and social action. 'Traditional' sociology seemed immured within a rational-scientific perspective which operated with a fact–value distinction that appeared out of tune with contemporary needs for political action, and appeared to have few answers to these issues.

It is against such a backdrop that various forms of Marxism and 'critical theory' come to the fore. The centrality of praxis-based approaches to the political perspective is a result of the idea that sociology is a component of society's reflection upon itself: in other words, acting upon the social world to change it might be done in order to know something about its underlying mechanisms. As a result, sociology becomes predominantly an inherently 'reflexive' discipline, which has a duty to link its intellectual processes to questions of social change.

A classic and still influential formulation of this argument was made by **Alvin Gouldner** in a book written at the end of the 1960s, *The Coming Crisis of Western Sociology* (1970) that appeared to presage a fundamental break with the non-reflexive sociologies he associated with conservative traditions in social thought. One of these was the then dominant paradigm of US sociology – functionalism – which he identified as emerging from the work of Talcott Parsons. But Gouldner also directed strong critical attention to the 'state Marxism' of the Communist bloc as another form of conservative theory about society. A little earlier, Gouldner had outlined some of the reasons why he was developing a radical movement away from 'rational–scientific' sociology in his attack on value freedom as a 'myth' (Gouldner, 1962).

Gouldner, Alvin

The sentiments expressed by Gouldner in *The Coming Crisis of Western Society* and presaged by his critique of 'value free' sociology seem to have influenced a large swathe of sociology in the period after his book was written, but for reasons perhaps not always linked to his own work. It might have seemed that while he was concerned with a more general issue within the discipline, those who took up sociology were doing so precisely because they saw it as a means of effecting social change.

Nowhere is this clearer, perhaps, than in the feminist movement, as we see in more detail in section 4.3. The emergence of a feminist sociology in the 1970s appears as part of a wider set of changes in social, philosophical, political and psychological ideas about gender roles and sexuality more generally. Central to feminism's social programme was the notion that sociology could be a vital weapon in ensuring that the social changes it aimed at could be instituted. But feminist thinking could not proceed, many argued, unless it could sweep away the epistemological bases of 'masculinist thinking'. As Terry Lovell has argued,

> The challenge of contemporary feminist theory has necessarily taken it into the heart of the most intractable questions of the nature of knowledge itself. The first move which has had to be made within each discipline has been to deconstruct what has passed for knowledge so as to expose its masculinist perspective and associated exclusions. The second has often quickly followed the first, that of advancing either strong claims for 'women's knowledge' or perhaps more cautious affirmations of the possibilities of 'feminist standpoint epistemology'.
>
> (Lovell, 1996, p.335)

As Lovell argues, the feminist approach within social theory is resolutely devoted to challenging the truth-claims of masculinist epistemologies. In this sense it provides a neat picture of one of the major consequences of the political perspective in sociology, for if social or political aspirations are considered to be central elements of the sociological enterprise itself, then knowledge creation must also be seen as subservient to these aspirations. This has, in turn, led feminists and other social theorists to argue that all knowledge creation is socially relative or contextual, contingent upon the viewpoint or social position of the thinker. This is essentially the position taken by Foucault and also many post-modernist thinkers, who have increasingly seen the activity of writing about society as a form of knowledge creation in its own right – one that can have important consequences for analysing and reconstructing social phenomena.

We have looked at the 'political perspective' within sociology as one which insists upon sociologists recognizing the socially embedded nature of their work, and the consequent impossibility of the sort of 'value freedom' that is so much a concern of the rational-scientific perspective.

Because the typical issues tackled by such uses of sociology are so closely linked to the perceived need to effect one form of social change or another, it may be appropriate to describe them as 'relativist', in the sense that they present the researcher with entirely specific or 'relative' forms of knowledge creation. Feminist theory, as pointed out, has been primarily concerned with 'challenging the truth-claims of masculinist epistemologies'. Although political theories and positions may be thought of as forms of 'relativism' because of their particularism and bias in favour of specific interests, they often contain the assumption that the specificity of their approach, and particularly their attention to the need to 'open up' hitherto concealed or repressed areas of knowledge, will lead to a more inclusive epistemology in which the particular interests they promote receive wider attention.

But there is another 'relativist' perspective which we should now examine. It is less frequently 'political' in scope, and has placed even greater emphasis on meaning and on the style in which sociological thought is expressed. It is what we have termed 'sociology as theory'.

3.3 The 'sociology as theory' perspective

The 'sociology as theory', or sociology for its own sake, perspective sees its purpose as engaging intellectually with society in a descriptive way. Its primary role is thus to describe the world for its own sake and to provide knowledge about the social world rather than to seek to organize society better or to change it politically (Figure 4.2). Sociology and literature are often thought to be uneasy bedfellows. Yet some of the most interesting and well-known sociological writing has become famous because it offers narrative thrust and imaginative characterization. For example, a number of community studies fall into this category: Whyte's *Street Corner Society* (1961, first published 1943) and Willmott and Young's *Family and Kinship in East London* (1957) are iconic examples (these are discussed further in, for example, Chapters 3 and 6 of *Understanding Everyday Life,* see **Hamilton, 2002,** and **Jordan, 2002**).

Figure 4.2 *Students and staff attending a university lecture: the 'sociology as theory' perspective is interested in the production of sociological knowledge for its own sake*

One of the most interesting writers on sociological matters has been Erving Goffman, whose work was referred to earlier. Gouldner, for instance, called him 'the William Blake of sociology' (Gouldner, 1962). Goffman's 'dramaturgical' approach to the 'play-acting' involved in social situations is at its most intriguing when he discusses the simple processes of social interaction that we might see anywhere, at any time. As suggested earlier in the chapter, a classic is his analysis of 'couple tie-signs' – the symbolic markers, such as hand-holding, that couples use to signal to the rest of the world that they are just that. For instance, Goffman wrote:

> Having begun to learn about the meaning of hand-holding by looking at those who do it and those who don't, we can go forward. Given the people who do it, we can ask when it is they do it, and when it is they don't (when they might).

First, not doing it. There is a rule in formal etiquette that it is improper for couples to walk down the fashionable shopping streets of a city holding hands. There is another rule that married couples at social parties are supposed to 'mix' that is, to lay aside their excluding relationship temporarily so that they can be active simply in their capacity as members of the party. A corollary of this rule is that they are not supposed to hold hands. (They may hold hands on the way to the party and back from the party but not during the party.) It is also the case that although college students can walk on the campus holding hands – in fact that seems to be one of the special places for this sort of activity – they ought not to listen to lectures thusly encumbered. Furthermore, in some social establishments holding hands even outdoors is forbidden. In industrial schools for persons with a court charge, hand-holding may be prohibited within the gates, as it may be to nurse–physician pairs on the hospital grounds. In these latter cases, of course, whether for penal or professional reasons, the members must be so strictly disciplined that even when walking between buildings, a high orientation to the purposes of the establishment must be maintained. (As may be expected, other [similar practices] such as smoking may also be prohibited.) It appears, then, that when much of an individual's orientation and involvement is necessary, hand-holding may have to be forborne along with other acts through which the mutual involvement of the closely related might be thrust upon the public at large.

The significance of this discipline will be emphasised if we look at situations where hand-holding seems to be approved and even idealised. In our pictorial world of advertising and movies – if not in the real world – vacationing couples are featured walking down crooked little streets in foreign places holding hands. At issue here is the fact that tourists often feel they do not owe the business streets of foreign societies the deference these places often demand from locals; tourists can therefore withdraw, just as they can wear informal clothing. Further, the very foreignness of the place suggests a slight exposure, if not fear, and, for the woman at least, holding the hand of the one she is paired with is a pictured source of support. Magazine couples are also featured holding hands while walking barefooted (shoes in other hand) on the seashore. Here, obviously, the absence of civil society allows a greater withdrawal than might otherwise be tolerated, an undisguised mooning as it were, and the very empty reaches of the ocean might cause an anomic flutter nicely checked by the confirmation of a held hand.

(Goffman, 1972, pp.228–9)

As this suggests, and was suggested earlier in the chapter, while Goffman may be particularly interested in understanding the dynamics of social behaviour, he is not really interested in treating such behaviour as if it were something that can be analysed in a 'rational–scientific' manner. Nor does he wish to use this insight for political purposes. He is, instead, most interested in exploring the form of social expression that 'tie-signs' appear to denote. And his technique for examining them involves him in the use of entirely 'qualitative' methods: judgement, insight, empathy, and alertness to the implicit and fluid rules governing social behaviour. All of this is typical of what we term the 'sociology as theory' perspective within sociology.

'Sociology as theory' or sociology for its own sake has drawn increasingly on the so-called 'qualitative' methods, in contrast to the quantitative techniques employed in various forms of survey research that involve counting of some sort. What are termed ethnographic approaches have become widely used. As we saw in Chapter 2, ethnographers immerse themselves in a society to collect descriptive data (via fieldwork) concerning the culture of its members from the perspective of the meanings members of that society attach to their social world; they then render the collected data intelligible and significant to fellow academics and other readers.

The ethnographer is part insider, a participant in the social world that is the object of investigation; and part outsider, since, although prior frameworks are to be eschewed in favour of contaminating the field of observation as little as possible, the results of the fieldwork must be transmitted to professional (and other) audiences and thereby interpreted in the context of frameworks that bestow credibility on the fieldwork. This last point means that the fieldwork must be written and indeed it is significant in this context that the term 'ethnography' is frequently employed to refer to the written account that is the product of ethnographic research. As one writer has put it: 'ethnography is something you may do, study, use, read or write' (Bryman, 2001, p.x).

As noted in Chapter 2, much of ethnography deals with meanings and symbolic processes: it is often used to attempt to interpret non-Western cultures, or to understand the behaviour of 'sub-cultural' groups within, say, Western societies (and this is why it is a mode of expression also widely used by anthropologists). This has long raised pertinent issues about how (and whether) meanings can be 'universalized' through the interpretative process. Increasingly, this process has been seen as essentially a question of how the work is written. Indeed its 'universalization' would often be taken as problematic, and many practitioners of this approach would see themselves as producing highly 'relative' and specific accounts, rather than material which would form part of a wider understanding of social processes. The creative process of writing thus becomes the object of the game.

ACTIVITY I

Imagine a debate between a sociologist sympathetic to the political perspective and a sociologist drawing on the 'sociology as theory' perspective. What do you think their differences might be? Make notes to clarify your thoughts.

The sociologist from the political perspective might insist that:

1   Sociologists should recognize the socially embedded nature of their work.

2   The role of sociologists is to try to change society.

3   Sociologists are embedded in relations of power.

4   Sociologists should even be activists themselves to inform their research and sociological understanding.

The sociologist who is sympathetic to the 'sociology as theory' perspective might argue that:

1   There is no need per se for sociologists to change the world.

2   There is a relatively thin line between sociology and literature.

3   Ethnographic research is a useful approach to understanding other cultures.

SUMMARY OF SECTION 3

1   One way to think about the purposes of sociology is in terms of the competing perspectives: the rational-scientific, political and 'sociology as theory'.

2   The rational–scientific perspective:

   ■ engages with the idea of 'value freedom' or, at least, value neutrality

   ■ engages with the notion that 'society' has an objective, independent existence and the main purpose of sociology is to find out the truth about it

   ■ often uses a model for sociology, which is akin to that of the natural sciences, such as physics.

3   The political perspective is based on the notions that:

   ■ value freedom is a myth and sociology always involves value judgements (as Gouldner argued)

   ■ sociology is fundamentally different from the natural sciences because 'society' – the object of sociological study – is fundamentally different from nature

   ■ sociology is concerned with changing the world.

4   The 'sociology as theory' perspective:

   ■ concentrates on the meaning of social experience, rather than emphasizing scientific knowledge or political utility

   ■ emphasizes relativity, but also suggests that sociology is an attempt to impose some form of meaning on the flux of human affairs

   ■ stresses the literary or rhetorical construction of sociological work.

4   The uses of sociology

Having considered how sociologists have perceived the purposes of the discipline, we now turn to some examples of how sociology has impacted on the world – that is, how sociological knowledge has been put to practical use. There are countless arenas in which sociological knowledge has been deployed and here we look at three: in government; in commercial life; and by social movements – notably the feminist movement.

4.1   Sociology and government

One key arena in which sociology has played an important role is in the field of government. Two different examples of this relationship are considered here. First, sociological ideas have, at various historical junctures, had an important influence on the thinking of governments. This may be at one step removed or it may involve the active participation of sociologists in the construction of the political agenda, as we shall see in the example of New Labour's 'third way'. The second issue addressed, that of social statistics, is an example of more complex ways in which sociological categories actively shape the social world and interventions in it (the discussion that follows utilizes material drawn from **Bennett, 2002**; the authors gratefully acknowledge his permission for its use).

The social agendas of the third way

The ideas behind different political parties' agendas and policies have historically owed a great deal to ideas generated by sociologists. A good illustration of this took place in the first years of Tony Blair's New Labour government which articulated a new political platform, the third way, which was posed as an alternative to previous forms of politics – both left and right. Central to this strategy were the writings of Anthony Giddens (Figure 4.3), formerly Director of the London School of Economics and Political Science, and, prior to that, Professor of Sociology at the University of Cambridge. As

Figure 4.3 *Anthony Giddens*

Allbrow suggests 'British sociologists must take satisfaction in the influence that Anthony Giddens has enjoyed as the world spokesman for the Third Way' (2001, p.10). In doing so, Albrow is highlighting the fact that these new symbiotic relations between sociology and government have become publicly visible in distinctive ways through the high profile of Giddens and his close relationship with Blair. As the author of *The Third Way: The Renewal of Social Democracy* (1998) and its sequel *The Third Way and its Critics* (2000), Giddens has enjoyed a public prominence unrivalled by any contemporary British intellectual and without parallel in the history of British sociology.

As an alternative to strategies that had gone before, the third way was an attempt to redraw the political map, to redefine where the political right, left and centre are, and to do so in a way that allowed the third way to emerge not as a middle way but as a new centrist political programme that could, at the same time, claim to be radical. The third way thus sought to redefine the very space of politics, to declare the traditional divisions of left and right outmoded, and to place itself at the centre of a new way of mapping both political space (the left–right spectrum) and time (the division, for example, between Old and New Labour). This was a political programme which was driven by its responsiveness to social change. As Giddens puts it:

> I shall take it 'third way' refers to a framework of thinking and policy-making that seeks to adapt social democracy to a world which has changed fundamentally over the past two or three decades. It is a third way in the sense that it is an attempt to transcend both old-style social democracy and neoliberalism.
>
> (Giddens, 1998, p.26)

Thus, Giddens portrays traditional social democracy and neoliberalism as diametrically opposed on some issues (for example, the relations between the state and civil society) while sharing common ground on others (for instance, both support linear modernization and have a low ecological consciousness). This allows him to depict the third way as something that transcends these political programmes in two overlapping but nonetheless significantly different ways. In the first, the third way comes to the rescue in proposing a better balance between the polarized and unacceptable extremes represented by old-style social democracy and neoliberalism. Rather than advocating too much or too little state power, allowing too much or too little influence to the operation of markets, or granting communities too much or too little power, the third way gets it 'about right'. In the second strategy, however, the third way emerges not as a sensible alternative to polarized extremes but as something that goes beyond both old-style social democracy and neoliberalism in respect of the ground they share: their low ecological consciousness, for example. As previously suggested, Giddens's thinking about the third way has had a direct influence on New Labour's ideas and, indeed, its policies (Figure 4.4). As such, Giddens's work provides a prominent example fo the way in which sociology can and does shape politics and government.

Figure 4.4 *Tony Blair greets the crowds outside Downing Street in the wake of the 1997 Labour election victory*

Social statistics

While Giddens's work provides an example of the way in which sociology impacts directly on politics and government, the history of social statistics suggests a more complex relationship between sociological knowledge and government, one that is, in consequence, arguably more profound. Sociology has a long history of involvement with government and social administration in the UK, beginning with the collection of social statistics in the nineteenth century and continuing in the development of the welfare state.

In commenting on this history, Ian Hacking (1991) has argued that the development of statistics has: 'helped determine the form of laws about society and the character of social facts'; 'engendered concepts and classifications within the human sciences'; and 'created ... a great bureaucratic machinery'. According to Hacking, if it weren't for the power of statistics, it is possible you would not exist, given the overwhelming likelihood that our nineteenth-century forebears would not have lived to puberty. This is a graphic illustration of his argument that statistics may be malevolent or benign, depending on the nature of the governmental programmes and rationalities that regulate their use.

But Hacking also emphasizes the role of statistics in making society thinkable in certain ways. The view of what can count as a social fact today is certainly broader than that proposed by Durkheim, but it is still true that the ability to demonstrate law-like regularities of behaviour on the part of those occupying similar social positions remains a powerful aspect of the uses of sociology. It is, for example, still important in assessing the different life-chances that are associated with different class positions (see **Savage, 2002**). But we can also see how the frameworks in which statistical data are collected are productive ones, in the sense that, by making certain kinds of social division statistically visible in particular ways, they can generate unforeseen consequences. Hacking thus suggests that the emergence of Marx's class analysis and the subsequent development of class politics can be understood, at least in part, as something generated by the categories used in the census. The use of racially or ethnically derived principles of classification for the collection of statistical data has had similar consequences, often contributing significantly to a racialization of social divisions (see **Murji, 2002**). In short, the example of social statistics suggests that sociological knowledge can itself become a technical instrument of government and social administration, one that actively *shapes* the social world it purports only to describe.

4.2   Commercial uses of sociological knowledge

Another area in which sociological forms of knowledge have been put to use in a manner suggesting that sociology actively shapes the social world as much as it reflects it, is to be found in the field of commerce and labour markets (the following utilizes material drawn from **McFall, 2002**; the authors gratefully acknowledge her permission for its use). There has been a number of different attempts to apply sociology and the social sciences to restructure and reform the workplace to the mutual advantage of worker satisfaction and company profitability. In many of these attempts the objective has been to develop new techniques and processes to transform workers' subjective experience of the workplace.

As this suggests, there is considerable overlap between sociology that seeks to study the operation of the economy and sociology that has been applied in order to improve its operation. For instance, Weber's model of bureaucracy had a major impact on the ways in which economic organizations were structured throughout the twentieth century. Weber's work on bureaucracy was multi-faceted and sought to provide an analysis and a critique of some of its effects. It was not his aim to provide a blueprint upon which large organizations could model themselves; nevertheless, his work has been widely appropriated in this way. In particular, his emphasis on the establishment of a clear and formalized hierarchy in which the principles of order, authority and responsibility can be instilled has had a huge impact upon management theory.

At about the time that Weber was writing, Frederick Taylor's proposals were also coming to the fore. Taylor advocated the establishment of a 'science' of management based on the minute analysis and measurement of different work tasks. Although quite distinct in approach and focus – Weber concentrated on delineating the responsibilities of the manager, while Taylor addressed the tasks of the worker – both shared an enthusiasm for a formalized approach to economic organization. This 'formalization' involved a dehumanization of work. As Weber commented, organizations 'develop more perfectly the more bureaucracy is dehumanised' (1948, p.215). Moreover, Weber – although critical of some of its effects – believed Taylor's methods would contribute to the 'rational conditioning…of work performances' (Weber, 1948, p.261).

Unsurprisingly, both these approaches have met with criticism over the years. The idea that dehumanizing and de-skilling work processes would produce widespread rationalization has been far from universally accepted and many have balked at the human costs in terms of monotony, boredom and the suppression of creativity at work. In addition, both approaches have been regarded as symptomatic of the need of management, in capitalist modes of economic organization, to exert increasing control over the workplace. Rose (1999), however, has argued that these managerial approaches should not be understood simply as a function of the inexorable drive of capitalism, but as part of a broader series of programmes in which new techniques and forms of knowledge were applied in an attempt to improve national efficiency. Taylorism, Rose argues, shared with other programmes:

> … a belief in the improvement of individuals through the application of expertise. … [I]t did this by constructing norms and standards that accorded a visibility to previously obscure and unimportant aspects of the activities of persons, and by calibrating and governing these minutiae of existence in accordance with these norms …

> (Rose, 1999, p.59)

Taylor's concerns with 'fitting the job to the man and the man to the job', for instance, also preoccupied the occupational psychologist Charles Myers. Myers rejected Taylor's mechanistic approach to workers and he argued that industry had to take into consideration the 'complex subjective life' of workers. This was to be achieved by managing the 'mental atmosphere of the work' through management style and the satisfaction of worker interests (Rose, 1999, p.69).

The emphasis on 'mental hygiene' as the key to industrial efficiency was complemented at about the same time by the development in the United States of what became known as the Human Relations School of Management. Human Relations is associated with the work of Elton Mayo. Mayo's initial concern had been with the effects of work-breaks, light and environmental conditions on productivity. He put these factors to the test in a now famous series of investigations at the Hawthorne Electric Works in the 1920s. The Hawthorne investigations involved some 20,000 'non-directed interviews'. In the course of these interviews the researchers became increasingly conscious of the subjective, emotional significance to the worker of particular events in the workplace. From these data the researchers developed a view of the factory as a social organization in which conflict arose not as a result of the objectively alienating nature of the work, as in the Marxist account, nor as an outcome of individual maladjustment, as in Myers' mental hygiene approach. Rather, conflict here was construed as a result of the different values of different groups in the organization. Management's concern with cost and efficiency, for example, might frequently be at odds with workers' attachment to established ways of doing things (Rose, 1999). The Human Relations approach to workplace management that arose from this research advocated that study of the values and practices of different groups would promote organizational harmony and therefore efficiency:

> The task of management was to manage the enterprise and change within it in light of a knowledge of the values and sentiments of the workforce, and to act upon these so as to make them operate for rather than against the interests of the firm.
>
> (Rose, 1999, p.72)

What we have seen in this section, then, is how sociological ideas concerning hierarchy, order, authority, precise and formal measurement of work tasks, and the impacts of working conditions, have had an important influence on the field of commerce. As with the example of social statistics, above, this suggests that sociology changes the world even in the process of describing it.

Figure 4.5 *Workers taking a coffee break: sociological studies of workplace cultures have given rise to various new management practices designed to improve commercial productivity and efficiency*

4.3   'The personal is political'

If the relationship between sociology and social action is a 'two way street' (with sociological knowledge both reflecting and actively shaping social action), it is perhaps unsurprising that some sociologists have rejected the idea that sociology should attempt to be value free or even value neutral (see the discussion in section 8.3 of Chapter 1), arguing instead that sociology is itself a form of political activism and that sociologists should be politically active in a wider sense. In section 3.2 we introduced the sociological perspective that embodies this idea, one that sees the role of sociology as being to bring about (or perhaps prevent) social change. The feminist movement of the late 1960s and 1970s (sometimes referred to as second-wave feminism) offers a good illustration of this.

To explore academic feminism's mutually constitutive relationship with political activism, as in Chapter 1, we are going to revisit material taken from elsewhere in DD201, in this case Linda Janes's discussion of second-wave feminism in **Braham and Janes (2002)**, reproduced here as Reading 4.1. From this reading we see that radical feminism, like socialist feminism, was developed in the context of a proliferation of feminist sociological writings which provided theoretical and empirical material to support the activist political movement where these ideas were put into practice.

READING 4.1

You should now read 'The personal is political' (Reading 4.1 at the end of this chapter). As you read, consider the following questions.

1   Why were socialist feminists and radical feminists drawn to different political struggles?

2   In what ways did second-wave feminism demonstrate a reciprocal relationship between sociology and social action?

To summarize, then, socialist feminists thought an analysis of gender divisions had to be integrated with an analysis of class divisions in order to understand the position of women in society, whereas radical feminists explained women's oppression primarily in terms of patriarchy. The different perspectives thus generated different forms of political engagement and activism. Socialist feminists tended to be involved in campaigns concerned with employment, economic inequality and education. Radical feminists were more likely to be involved with issues of sexuality, violence towards women and reproduction.

As this implies, feminist theory and writing fed very directly into feminist activism, through developing an understanding and analysis of the conditions of oppression and inequality that women experienced in the real world. At the same time, the experience of feminist activists in different political struggles was drawn upon by feminist sociologists to develop and extend their own theoretical ideas. The relationship between feminist sociology and feminist activism was thus a mutually constituted one.

SUMMARY OF SECTION 4

1   The relationship between sociology and the world is a mutually constituted one (that is, it is a two-way street).

2   The relationship of sociology to politics, government and commerce may be a simple one: sociologists are directly involved in politics, policy or commercial life; or a more complex one: sociological knowledge changes the world even as it describes it.

3   Sociological perspectives from a feminist perspective have been deeply implicated in the politics of second-wave feminism; and feminist activism, in turn, was fed back into sociological knowledge, opening up the field of feminist theory and gender studies.

5   Uses for twenty-first century sociology

In this final section we look at one well known sociologist's view concerning the role of sociology in the future. In a special symposium, *Charting Futures for Sociology* (published at the beginning of the new millennium), the official review journal of the American Sociological Association, *Contemporary Sociology*, invited the Australian sociologist R.W. Connell (Figure 4.6) to write the opening article. In this article, he begins by noting that it was not pre-ordained that sociology should have come into existence in the way that it did, and goes on to point out that it is not guaranteed that sociology will continue to exist unless it draws on new sources of experience and discovers new standpoints. The question he poses is whether there is a future for sociology if it is confined to being a 'reformist science' (providing useful expertise in carrying out surveys and making field observations in the form of small-scale ethnographies), or might there be more challenging futures? Your first reaction might (not unreasonably) be to think that there is nothing wrong with being reformist and useful. However, Connell is being true to what we might call the more 'prophetic' aspects of the sociological perspective (those that see sociology's role as being to identify and make recommendations about the future developments of sociology). As such, his arguments are certainly worthy of our attention.

Figure 4.6
R.W. Connell

Since the 1970s and into the opening years of the twenty-first century, market ideas and forces have become dominant throughout the world. In these circumstances, it has been suggested, sociology may be left with few functions. One is that of performing a kind of 'salvage ethnography' of marginalized life-styles – what Connell refers to disparagingly as similar to the old ethnographies of 'nuts, sluts, and perverts' (for an overview of the development of ethnography, see **Bennett and Watson, 2002**). Another possible function, according to Connell, for those who still want to affect the world, is for market-society sociology to be a science of the 'losers' – people who are poor, chronically sick, disturbed, violent; linguistic minorities, illiterate (including the computer illiterate) and unemployed people. None of these functions, however valuable in itself, seems to meet the challenge of working out a future for sociology that matches the comprehensive scope and critical edge of earlier sociological perspectives (although some professional sociologists may disagree and regard this, realistically and modestly, as no bad thing). To escape marginalization and slow decline, Connell argues, sociology must be 'reconstituted as a democratic science', which entails stepping outside the confines of the Western academic world and entering into partnerships with new participants.

Where are the new partnerships to be found? Among those mentioned as possible candidates are activists in various spheres of society – union organizers, teachers, broadcasters, community activists, and even some bureaucrats. Connell's more general point is that, in a knowledge-based society, knowledge is an important tool of social control, and so it is crucial to spread access to that tool, especially to those who are disadvantaged. Sometimes it is simply a case of revealing the salient facts about inequalities; in other cases it may involve giving a community group the tools to reveal the processes that have been obscured by ideology, for example with regard to the social construction of distinctions between normal and deviant sexualities, or exposing the sources of land pollution. Finally, sociology needs to broaden its perspectives to encompass non-Western intellectual resources. The latter presents, perhaps, the most difficult challenge, as it can come directly into conflict with deeply ingrained aspects of Western thought and values that can seem to be an inextricable part of the sociological heritage – notions of rationality and science or progress and modernity, for instance. What is being called for is a sociology that 'deconstructs' the binary opposites that have structured Western discourses, including some of sociology's own assumptions: Occidental/Oriental; modern/traditional; rational/emotional; and active/passive.

This call, for deconstructive strategies to expose the artifice involved in the construction of binaries in Western discourses and cultural identities, has also been applied to other oppositions such as male/female and heterosexual/homosexual. This is an important strategy for sociology to pursue, for sociology to be of use by different social groups such as the feminist movement, gay movement, national liberation movements and other social movements who want and need to position themselves differently in relation to dominant norms, discourses and practices. If sociology continues to push the boundaries and edges of knowledge, on the one hand, and conduct excellent research on the other, it will continue to be useful and to be used by practitioners, policy makers, politicians, employers, activists and others in the world outside academic sociology.

ACTIVITY 2

Looking back over this chapter and the rest of the course, jot down some ideas on what role you envisage sociology will play in the future.

You might have come up with all sorts of ideas, since none of us can predict what the future may bring. You may agree with the idea that sociology will be left with very few functions, or limited ones – such as the ethnography of marginalized life-styles. You may see sociology as playing an important political role in providing the social research needed to support people working with poor and marginalized groups to improve their lot. If you looked back at *Social Differences and Divisions*, in particular, you will have reminded yourself that there are many divisions and differences in society which are likely to continue to exist, in some cases possibly at an even more extreme level, which sociological research and knowledge can help us make sense of and, according to the political perspective, help change.

You may also agree with Connell that it is time that sociology broadens its perspective to encompass non-Western perspectives, values and discourses. This, you might think, represents a crucial new avenue that sociology should pursue. And finally you may also think that sociology can play an important part in the breaking down of old binaries in Western discourses and cultural identities, thus opening up new strategies for people involved in the various social movements. Whatever your thoughts on this, it is likely that there are many answers to the question of how sociology might develop over the next century.

SUMMARY OF SECTION 5

1　R.W. Connell argues that sociology needs to renew its purpose for the twenty-first century if it is to retain its role as a vital force in human affairs.

2　One of the most important strategies for renewal that Connell identifies is the need for sociology to reach out to new global constituencies; a second strategy is for sociology to 'deconstruct' the binaries underpinning its own and wider Western world views.

6　Conclusion

We have covered a lot of ground in this chapter, and you may have found it difficult to take it all in. You have been introduced to the three different perspectives within sociology on the relationship between sociological knowledge and the world 'out there'. You should now be able to distinguish these three main sociological perspectives – the rational–scientific, the political and the 'sociology as theory' – and their views on sociology's engagement with the social. As we have noted, different sociologists have different views on the purposes of sociology and the ways it can be used in the real world.

　　You have also looked in some detail at various ways in which sociology has been put to use in government, in commerce and in social movements (in particular, the feminist movement). You will have understood how sociological knowledge and social action are mutually constitutive, or to put this another way, sociology's engagement with the real world is a two-way process where each informs and constructs the other. Finally, we hope by now you may feel confident that there are some ways in which you can, in your own life, make use of the sociology you have studied in this course.

References

Albrow, M. (2001) 'Sociology after the Third Way, in the UK and USA', *Network* (the newsletter of the British Sociological Association), no.78, January, pp.10–12.

Alexander, J. (2001) 'Introduction', *Mainstream and Critical Social Theory*, London, Sage.

Baudrillard, J. (1986) *America*, Paris, Editions Du Seuil.

Bennett, A. (1994) *Writing Home*, London, Faber & Faber.

Bennett, T. (2002) 'Sociology and government' in Hamilton, P. and Thompson, K. (eds) *op cit*.

Bennett, T. and Watson, D. (2002) 'Introduction' in Bennett, T. and Watson, D. (eds) *op cit*.

Bennett, T. and Watson, D. (eds) (2002) *Understanding Everyday Life*, Oxford, Blackwell/The Open University.

Braham, P. and Janes, L. (eds) (2002) *Social Differences and Divisions*, Oxford, Blackwell/The Open University.

Bryman, A. (2001) *Ethnography*, London, Sage.

Giddens, A. (1998) *The Third Way: The Renewal of Social Democracy*, Cambridge, Polity Press.

Giddens, A. (2000) *The Third Way and its Critics*, Cambridge, Polity Press.

Goffman, E. (1972) *Interaction Ritual: Essays on Face to Face Behaviour*, Harmondsworth, Penguin.

Gouldner, A.W. (1962) 'Anti-minotaur: the myth of a value-free sociology', *Social Problems*, no.9, pp.199–213.

Gouldner, A. (1970) *The Coming Crisis of Western Sociology*, London, Heinemann.

Hacking, I. (1991) 'How should we do the history of statistics?' in Burchell, G., Gordon, C. and Miller, P. (eds), *The Foucault Effect*, London, Harvester/Wheatsheaf.

Hamilton, P. (2002) 'The street and everyday life' in Bennett, T. and Watson, D. (eds) *op. cit.*

Hamilton, P. and Thompson, K. (eds) (2002) *The Uses of Sociology*, Oxford, Blackwell/ The Open University.

Jordan, T. (2002) 'Community, everyday and space' in Bennett, T. and Watson, D. (eds) *op. cit.*

Lovell, T. (1996) 'Feminist social theory' in Turner, B.S. (ed.) *op. cit.*, pp.335–7.

McFall, L. (2002) 'Tools for commerce?' in Hamilton, P. and Thompson, K. (eds) *op. cit.*

Murji, K. (2002) 'Race, power and knowledge' in Braham, P. and Janes, L. (eds) *op. cit.*

Outhwaite, W. (1996) *Positivism and Sociology*, London, Allen & Unwin.

Robbins, D. (2000) *Bourdieu and Culture*, London, Sage.

Rose, N. (1999) *Governing the Soul* (2nd edn), London, Routledge.

Savage, M. (2002) 'Social exclusion and class analysis' in Braham, P. and Janes, L. (eds) *op. cit.*

Turner, B.S. (ed.) (1996) *The Blackwell Companion to Social Theory*, Oxford, Blackwell.

Weber, M. (1948) *From Max Weber: Essays in Sociology* (trans. and ed. Gerth, H.H. and Mills, C.W.) London, Routledge and Kegan Paul.

Reading

4.1 Linda Janes, 'The personal is political' (2002)

Modern feminism's second wave was … part of the wide social upheavals generated at the end of the 1960s, linked to the civil rights movement and student protests across Europe and the United States. The period between the 'first-wave' struggles for suffrage (women achieved full suffrage in Britain only in 1928) and the 'second-wave' resurgence of feminism in the late 1960s is typically, although not universally, reviewed as a regressive period for women's politics. The two World Wars had enormous impact, drawing women into waged labour to an unprecedented degree, and then returning them to the home in peacetime on the back of a hugely influential ideology of domestic and familial responsibility in the service of post-war reconstruction. In 1963, however, Betty Friedan's *The Feminine Mystique* identified a 'problem with no name' for women. Although this was primarily a liberal feminist text, it highlighted the malign social and psychological effects – previously little acknowledged and therefore 'un-nameable' – of middle-class women's economic dependency on men in the home. In the second wave the domestic sphere became the focus of feminist critical debate, located – albeit differently by socialist and radical feminists – as a key site of women's oppression. The development of the Women's Liberation Movement (WLM) at this time depended significantly on thinking generated through the medium of consciousness-raising groups, where women's sharing of personal experiences across the public/private divide galvanized a new politicized collective consciousness. The slogan 'the personal is political' became the condensed representative signifier of the second wave.

Many women involved in the WLM were also active in left politics at the time and, defining themselves as Marxist or socialist feminists, were concerned with the failure of class-based politics and theory to address or explain gender inequalities. Harriet Bradley highlights the theoretical difficulty, and the solution provided by socialist feminists:

> Marxist analysis tended to handle the issue of gender inequality either by seeing women as members of the exploited working class (which they are clearly all not) or as housewives contributing either directly or indirectly to capitalist profits (which again they are all not). Moreover, gender divisions were shown by comparative historical study to be characteristic of all societies, not just capitalist or even class-divided societies, and to be marked in the Soviet bloc where capitalism had been rejected. It became apparent that it was impossible to conceptualise gender adequately within the single framework of the capitalist mode of production.
>
> The solution taken by Marxist feminists was to combine an account of capitalism with an analysis of a parallel system of patriarchy. Sometimes this took the form of what was known as unified systems theory, discerning a single complex structure of capitalist patriarchy or patriarchal capitalism (Young, 1981). … However, there was a tendency in these accounts for gender issues to slide out of sight and class imperatives to come to the fore. For this reason most feminists preferred the 'dual systems' option, which conceives patriarchy and capitalism as two equivalent and analytically separable systems which, however, are always found in any concrete social context.
>
> (Bradley, 1996, pp.87–8)

Socialist feminists, then, accounted for women's inequality at the theoretical level through the systemic operation of capitalism and patriarchy, working in tandem. Given their location in relation to Marxism, socialist feminists tended to focus on women's economic inequalities, although there was a recognition that these were fundamentally linked across waged work and unpaid domestic work through the unequal sexual division of labour which pertained in both arenas, regulated by a patriarchal state. The notion of unpaid domestic labour may seem a commonplace understanding now but, as Sheila Rowbotham, one of the most influential socialist feminists writing at the time, observed in reminiscence in 1989: 'I remember when it was not obvious that housework was work – hence the initial excitement created by this assertion.'

…

At the political level socialist feminist campaigns thus became concentrated, in matters such as demands for nurseries, reproductive rights, education and skill training and against women's low pay and discrimination and harassment at work. The priority was to reduce women's inequality by restructuring society in ways that would allow them to participate in waged work on a more equal basis with men. Unlike liberals, socialist feminism advocated fundamental, revolutionary change. Academic socialist feminism produced a prodigious amount of literature supporting these arguments for change that revealed and analysed women's exploitation in particular contexts of paid and unpaid work. Ann Oakley's *Housewife* (1974) was a pioneering work which drew attention to the ways in which women's domestic unpaid work is devalued and invisible in relation to men's paid work and the influence this has on constructing women's subordination. Empirical feminist sociological research demonstrated the reproduction of women's inequality through the operation of vertical and horizontal gendered segregation at work. Arguments promoted by politicians and employers, as well as some social theorists, to justify women's concentration in part-time work in terms of 'fitting-in' with their domestic responsibilities and by their 'naturally' weaker identification with the waged workplace, were called into question by the evidence that women usually had no alternative in the absence of affordable childcare. In addition, the ideological association between women and part-time work was demonstrated to reinforce its link with low pay.

...

Whilst patriarchy was seen to operate in concert with capitalism in socialist feminist understandings of women's subordination, for radical feminists of the second wave patriarchy was identified as the primary source of women's oppression. Radical feminists were interested in explaining women's oppression, solely as women rather than as workers. They therefore focused on issues of sexuality, marriage, motherhood and domestic violence against women, aspects of women's intimate experiences in the private domain. In distinction from the liberal project of constructing an androgynous society in which women would be like men and therefore equal to them, radicals affirmed women's commonality and emphasized their difference from men. The celebration of women's commonality – 'a bond which cuts across all boundaries' (Whelehan, 1995, p.87) – is invoked by the 'sisterhood is powerful' slogan, the title of an early

radical feminist anthology by Robin Morgan (1970). Radical feminism prioritized politics above theorizing and sought to mobilize women at the grassroots level through consciousness-raising groups that eschewed hierarchical organization. It was a fundamentally revolutionary form of politics because of its focus on aspects of private experience which had never been seen as within the scope of politics before. In this respect it transformed understandings of what could be 'political' (Whelehan, 1995). It was therefore more controversial than socialist strands because more threatening to the status quo, particularly in its advocacy, in its most extreme forms, of women's personal and political separatism. It was this aspect of radicalism that was typically caricatured in the popular press. However, its emphasis on woman-centred culture led to the development of communes, businesses and women's festivals and its political strategies led to the establishment of rape crisis and women's aid centres and wider support networks. Radical feminism has therefore transformed the lives of many women in very real terms.

References

Bradley, H. (1996) *Fractured Identities: Changing Patterns of Inequality*, Cambridge, Polity Press.

Friedan, B. (1963) *The Feminine Mystique*, London, Victor Gollancz.

Morgan, R. (ed.) (1970) *Sisterhood is Powerful: An Anthology of Writings from the Women's Liberation Movement*, New York, Vintage Books.

Oakley, A. (1974) *Housewife*, London, Allen Lane.

Rowbotham. S. (1989) *The Past is Before Us: Feminism in Action since the 1960s*, London, Pandora Press.

Whelehan, I. (1995) *Modern Feminist Thought: From the Second Wave to Post-Feminism*, Edinburgh, Edinburgh University Press.

Young, I. (1981) 'Beyond the happy marriage: a critique of the dual systems theory' in Sargent, L. (ed.) *Women and Revolution: The Unhappy Marriage of Marxism and Feminism*, London, Pluto Press.

Source: **Braham, P. and Janes, L. (eds) (2002) pp.120–5**

Acknowledgements

Grateful acknowledgement is made to the following sources for permission to reproduce material in this book:

Figures

Figure 1.5: Courtesy of Diane Watson; *Figure 2.1:* © David Tothill. Courtesy of Ann Oakley; *Figure 2.2:* © Bettmann / Corbis; *Figure 2.3:* screen reproduced from The British Sociological Association website, www.britsoc.co.uk; *Figure 3.1:* screen reproduced from National Statistics Online. Crown copyright material is reproduced with the permission of HMSO; *Figure 3.3: (left)* Collection of Senate House Library, University of London. © Courtesy of Belinda Norman-Butler, *(right)* Courtesy of The Joseph Rowntree Foundation; *Figure 4.1:* Courtesy of The London School of Economics; *Figure 4.3:* © Nigel Stead. Courtesy of The London School of Economics; *Figure 4.4:* © Tim Rooke / Rex Features; *Figure 4.6:* Courtesy of Professor Robert Connell.

Tables

Tables 3.1 and 3.2: Office for National Statistics (2000) *Social Trends 30.* Crown copyright material is reproduced with the permission of HMSO.

Cover photographs

Front cover, top left: Mike Levers/The Open University; all other photos on front cover: © United National Photographers (UNP); back cover: PhotoDisc.

Every effort has been made to contact copyright holders, but if any has been inadvertently overlooked, the publishers will be pleased to make the necessary arrangements at the first opportunity.

Index